Edgar Cayce in Context

SUNY Series in Western Esoteric Traditions
David Appelbaum, Editor

Edgar Cayce in Context

The Readings:
Truth and Fiction

K. PAUL JOHNSON

State University of New York Press

Published by
State University of New York Press, Albany

© 1998 State University of New York

For information, address State University of New York Press, State University Plaza, Albany, N.Y. 12246

Production by M. R. Mulholland
Marketing by Fran Keneston

Library of Congress Cataloging-in-Publication Data

Johnson, K. Paul, 1953–
    Edgar Cayce in context : the Readings', truth and fiction / K. Paul Johnson.
        p. cm. — (SUNY series in Western esoteric traditions)
    Includes bibliographical references and index.
    ISBN 0-7914-3905-4 (hardcover : alk. paper). — ISBN 0-7914-3906-2 (pbk. : alk. paper)
        1. Cayce, Edgar, 1877–1945. Edgar Cayce readings.
    2. Parapsychology. 3. Cayce, Edgar, 1877–1945. 4. Clairvoyance.
    5. Medicine, Magic, mystic, and spagiric. I. Title. II. Series.
    BF1023.C37 1998
    133.8'092—dc21   97-48932
                                                   CIP

10 9 8 7 6 5 4 3 2 1

Contents

Illustrations

Acknowledgments

Many people were very generous with time and interest in this project. Charles Thomas Cayce, David Bell, Harmon Bro, Mark Thurston, David Lane, Kym Smith, and Mary Graham all read the manuscript in full and provided useful advice for revision. Every suggestion made by these readers has been utilized to the best of my ability; remaining weaknesses in the book are my own. Edgar Evans Cayce, Paul and Walene James, Ken Butler, Chris Chandler, Larry Androes, Michael and Brenda Dougherty, and Charlotte Anderson read portions of the manuscript and provided helpful feedback. In conversations with Charles Thomas Cayce, Harmon Bro, David Bell, Paula Fitzgerald, Kirk Nelson, Pamela Van Allen, Grace Knoche, and Kirby Van Mater, I was given useful perspectives on the Edgar Cayce readings. I especially want to thank my cousins Carol Garrison, Doris Agee, Robert Rice, and Patricia Thompson for sharing their memories of Virginia Beach in the 1930s and '40s.

Postmodern readers may wish to know something of an author's biases at the outset, so I offer here a brief disclosure of my background and approach. My intention in this book is to provide a fair, balanced, sympathetic but objective introduction to the readings. In Tidewater Virginia, where I was born and reared, Edgar Cayce is regarded by many locals as an adopted native son. As a child I heard only good things about him; my Virginia Beach cousins had known Cayce as a family friend and remembered him fondly as a kind, unpretentious man who was beloved by the neighborhood children. The first book about him that I read, *Edgar Cayce on ESP*, was written by my cousin Doris Agee when I was a teenager. I belonged to the A.R.E. for a year in 1977–78 before focusing most of my attention on Theosophy for the next two decades. As an adult I have been influenced by the readings' guidelines on health and meditation, and participated in three Search for God groups at widely-spaced intervals. In 1995 I renewed membership in the A.R.E., but have never been involved in the organization apart from study group participation. Neither an insider nor an outsider, I can perhaps best be described as a "skeptical believer" in Cayce (as in Blavatsky, subject of my previous books). Balancing sympathy with objectivity entails a struggle to keep one's perception of facts uncontaminated by one's appreciation for the person or movement studied. The cost of such ambivalence is finding oneself condemned as too skeptical by believers and too credulous by skeptics. But this can be outweighed by the benefit of seeing possibilities that are unrecognized by partisans on either side of a polarized debate. I am a public librarian without advanced degrees in any academic discipline, and take a generalist's approach to the readings. My scholarly specialty is in the history of esoteric and metaphysical movements in the late nineteenth and early twentieth centuries in the English-speaking world. To be fully qualified for appraising the Cayce readings, one would need scholarly expertise in medicine, theology, psychology, and parapsychology; as a layman in all these fields I can offer only an overview of the major issues that deserve (and have in some cases received) deeper investigation by more qualified scholars.

It has been encouraging, in the wake of outraged Theosophical reactions to my earlier books, to discover the open-minded, nondefensive attitudes of A.R.E. leaders and authors regarding questions about Cayce's accuracy and sources. Charles Thomas Cayce, Edgar Evans Cayce, Mark Thurston, and Harmon Bro have been generous not just with helpful advice but also in their willingness to consider seriously the positions advanced in the following pages, skeptical or innovative though they may be. On the skeptical side of the equation, David Bell and David Lane have helped to prevent my enthusiasm for Cayce from undermining my objectivity, and have devoted as much time and energy to advising on the manuscript as the A.R.E.-affiliated persons named above.

I thank everyone who has shared in the evolution of this book, including the SUNY Press editors whose care and interest have been a steady encouragement. I thank the Edgar Cayce Foundation for permission to quote from the readings, and Jeanette Thomas for her assistance in this regard. The staff and volunteers of the A.R.E. Library were unfailingly helpful, and I particularly thank Claudeen Cowell and Alan Smith for their assistance.

I.1.

Thanksgiving dinner scene, 1937. Clockwise from left: Lucille Kahn, Gertrude Cayce, Edgar Cayce, Mary Sugrue, David E. Kahn, S. David Kahn, Hugh Lynn Cayce, Gladys Davis, Thomas Sugrue.

Photograph courtesy of the Edgar Cayce Foundation. Copyrighted 1978 Edgar Cayce Foundation. All rights reserved. Used by permission.

Introduction

Edgar Cayce's life and teachings uncannily recapitulate those of the founders of major American-born religious movements. Like Joseph Smith, prophet of Mormonism, Cayce experienced an angelic visitation in his youth, was recognized as psychically gifted by his family from an early age, and conveyed a new view of history derived from records that only he could see and read. Cayce's Kentucky home was in a region powerfully affected by the revivalism of the early nineteenth century, as was the "burnt-over district" of upstate New York where Mormonism was born. A crucial turning point in Cayce's life was his own miraculous healing that led to a commitment to healing others; in this he parallels Mary Baker Eddy, "discoverer" of Christian Science, whose emphasis on the influence of the mind on health is echoed in the Cayce readings. Like Ellen G. White, chief founder of the Seventh-day Adventists, Cayce combined a Bible-centered world view with a strong emphasis on diet and health; both received their revelations in a trance state and synthesized the alternative health systems of their eras. Cayce restored belief in reincarnation to a Western consciousness that had long since forgotten it; his most important precursor in this role was Theosophy's Madame Blavatsky, whose teachings find many parallels in the Cayce readings. Nevertheless, Cayce has yet to be recognized as a pivotal figure in American religious history as have Smith, White, Eddy, and to a lesser extent Blavatsky. The Association for Research and Enlightenment founded by Cayce and his associates has never promoted an independent religious identity comparable to Mormonism, Christian Science, Adventism, or Theosophy. Instead, it encourages its members of various faiths to remain in their folds while applying the spiritual wisdom and practical guidance found in the Cayce "readings." Cayce's influence has thereby permeated the inchoate milieu known as the New Age Movement, without crystallizing into ecclesiastical forms. Equally distinctive is the fact that virtually all of Cayce's voluminous body of work, which at 49,000 pages far exceeds any of the abovementioned spiritual leaders, was produced in a trance state of which he denied all memory. Rather than crafting a single message to humanity at large or to his followers, Cayce gave one message ("reading") at a time, more than

14,500 by the end of his life, the great majority to individuals. More than two-thirds of these were medical readings on a wide variety of ailments. Life readings providing spiritual and psychological advice as well as information about previous incarnations account for fourteen percent of the total. Business questions were answered in five percent of the readings, and another four percent gave dream interpretations for individuals.[1] Among the remaining miscellaneous readings were many answering questions from Cayce's co-workers concerning goals and methods of implementing his ideals in organizational form, which are now known as the "work" readings. As a result of the readings' specificity, it has taken years of effort to derive generally applicable principles from the mass of personal advice.

Measured by the objective standard of his literary presence, Cayce's historical significance is immense. As of May 1997, there were 123 entries in *Books in Print* (U.S.) under the subject of Cayce, compared to ninety-three for Joseph Smith, sixty for Mary Baker Eddy, forty-three for Helena Blavatsky, and thirty-three for Ellen G. White. A search of the WorldCat online database, which with thirty-six million bibliographic records is as near-exhaustive as can be found, yields comparable results. As of May 1997, there had been 646 books on the subject of Edgar Cayce published since 1950, compared to 547 on Ellen G. White, 542 on Joseph Smith, 264 on Mary Baker Eddy, and 121 on Helena Blavatsky. Yet as of the same date, Dissertation Abstracts Online shows only two entries on Cayce, compared to forty-four for White, twenty-six for Smith, and thirteen each for Blavatsky and Eddy. The relative fecundity of Cayce as a literary subject is even more striking when the 30,000 member Association for Research and Enlightenment is juxtaposed against the Mormons and Adventists, with around nine million members each, or the Christian Scientists with several hundred thousand. Theosophy, almost twice as old as the A.R.E., has approximately the same membership, yet its primary founder has generated many fewer books than Cayce. He has exerted a literary influence out of all proportion to the membership of the Association he founded, and comparable to the greatest religious innovators of the last two centuries in America. This makes it all the more surprising that scholarly interest in him has been so late in developing.

Perhaps because of his marked differences from spiritual leaders who consciously produced new religious movements, Cayce has not yet received much recognition and analysis from scholars of religious history. He has been pigeonholed as a "psychic," often regarded by friends and debunkers alike more as a case study in paranormal phenomena than as a pioneering religious thinker and synthesizer. The goal of this book is to initiate consideration of Cayce in historical context as a major figure in twentieth-century American spirituality. Each chapter explores a different aspect of his work. While "psychic" does describe Cayce accurately in some regards, in other dimensions of his work he might better be labeled as theosopher, mystic, occultist, healer, counselor, and prophet. In his dissertation and his biography of Cayce, Harmon Bro argues persuasively for "seer" as the most satisfactory term to describe him.

The perceived value of Cayce's output has been enhanced in some ways and diminished in others by the form in which it appeared. The implicit message of the readings' individual specificity is that God (or the Creative Forces) cares about and understands each person, and can provide cures for all ills of body, mind, or spirit. The New Age movement is marked by a hunger for specific personal guidance and spiritual connection, which Cayce's readings provide in greater detail than any of his predecessors or contemporaries. On the other hand, his literary legacy has required greater labors on the part of Cayce's successors than would have been necessary with a more traditional kind of teaching. The readings contain many inspiring and beautiful passages, but are often repetitive, murky, and convoluted; this seems characteristic of "channeled" material produced in a trance state. The best-known literary works resulting from Cayce's gifts have been by others, most notably the engaging biography *There Is a River,* by Thomas Sugrue. Many compilations and commentaries have been written over the years, but until recently the Cayce legacy has been rather impoverished from the point of view of primary source materials. The *Edgar Cayce Library Series,* a twenty-four-volume collection of verbatim extracts from the readings, was published mainly in the 1980s, and was the first large-scale publication of the readings. In the early 1990s, the entire collection of recorded readings from 1923 through 1944 was published in CD-ROM format, combined with background correspondence and follow-up reports. Not until 1996 was there a single-volume compendium of Cayce readings on the full range of topics they address. Conditions for scholarly study of Cayce are therefore more promising than they have been in the past.

Who Was Cayce?

Edgar Cayce was born March 18, 1877, on a farm near Beverly in Christian County, Kentucky, the only son of Leslie and Carrie Cayce. Leslie, locally known as "The Squire," was a small landowner who served as justice of the peace. Carrie also gave birth to four daughters, Ola, Sarah, Annie, and Mary. The family belonged to the Disciples of

Christ (Christian) Church, in which Edgar showed interest at an early age; at ten he became sexton in the Old Liberty Church.

Edgar was thirteen when his first indication of a spiritual calling appeared. He had developed a fascination with the Bible which would continue throughout his life; by his thirteenth birthday he had already read it through a dozen times.[2] In May 1890, while reading the Bible in the woods near his home, he had a vision which was later described in a memoir typed by Cayce himself:

> there was a sudden humming sound out side and bright light fill the little place where eddy sat, and a figure all in white bright as the noon day light, and the figure spoke—saying your prayers have been heard, what would you ask of me, that I may give it to you,— just that I may be helpful to others, especially to children who are ill, and that I may love my fellow man. and the figure was gone.[3]

This passage provides evidence of the limits of Cayce's literacy, which tends to be obscured by editing in the readings or correspondence that he dictated to secretaries; his education ended with the eighth grade. The next day he was distracted and inattentive at school, and performed so poorly in a spelling test that the teacher, his uncle Lucian, talked to the Squire about the need to enforce study discipline on the young dreamer. Edgar's father tried to drill him in spelling, but was so frustrated with the results that he knocked him to the floor. At that moment, Edgar heard the angelic being say, "If you can sleep a little, we can help you."[4] He took a short nap, and awoke with a photographic knowledge of the entire book, astounding his father by his sudden mastery of the previously hopeless spelling lesson. Cayce's biographers report that he slept with the speller as a pillow, but this detail is not found in his memoirs. Two years later, another strange ability manifested itself when Edgar was struck on the spine by a baseball. This caused a period of delirious behavior, which caused his father to put him to bed early. There he dictated instructions for a poultice which, he promised, would cure him by morning. His parents were delighted but bewildered when he awoke well but with no recollection of his previous disorder.[5]

After leaving school at fifteen, Edgar went to work on the farm of a cousin, but a year later accompanied his family to Hopkinsville, the county seat. There he worked in a bookstore and later as a shoe salesman in a dry goods store. In 1897, he began a long engagement to Gertrude Evans that ended with their marriage in 1903. From 1898 through 1900, he worked in a bookstore in Louisville and came home to Hopkinsville on weekends to visit his fiancee. At twenty-three, in 1900, he took a job based in Hopkinsville, selling insurance door to door. Soon an illness caused him to lose his voice, and he was obliged to give up his work as a salesman. In Hopkinsville on March 31, 1901, he first showed the remarkable ability that would bring him world-wide fame. Hypnotized by Al C. Layne, a bookkeeper who studied osteopathy by mail order, Edgar diagnosed his own malady: "In the normal state, this body is unable to speak, due to a partial paralysis of the inferior muscles of the vocal cords, produced by nerve strain. This is a psychological condition producing a physical effect. This may be removed by increasing the circulation to the affected parts by suggestion while in this unconscious condition."[6] Layne made the proposed suggestion, and as Edgar's parents watched, they saw his throat redden, and then heard him say, "The condition is removed. Make the suggestion that the circulation return to normal, and that after that the body awaken."[7] Edgar awoke with his voice restored, after ten months of silence, and began his career as a medical clairvoyant. His vocal paralysis returned several times and further hypnotic treatments brought relief. Cayce gave readings for other patients of Layne's, in 1902 effecting a remarkable cure of Aimee Dietrich, daughter of a prominent local citizen. In 1903, he married Gertrude and they settled in Bowling Green where he continued his career as a photographer. Four years later they had a son, Hugh Lynn, and in 1909, Cayce went to Alabama alone to practice photography, leaving his wife and son in Kentucky. On a return visit to Hopkinsville, Cayce's father introduced him to Dr. Wesley Ketchum, a homeopath who had recently opened a practice there. Ketchum tested Cayce's ability at clairvoyant diagnosis, and was sufficiently impressed to report the results to the *New York Times,* which on October 9, 1910, published a story headed (inaccurately) "Illiterate man becomes a doctor when hypnotized."[8] Unbeknownst to Cayce, Ketchum had previously described his abilities in a report written for a medical fraternity convention in Boston, and thus began the process that would lead quickly to national fame. The *Times* story was reprinted in newspapers across the country, and what had heretofore been a gift used occasionally was to become a lifelong preoccupation. Cayce moved back to Hopkinsville and in partnership with Ketchum became a psychic diagnostician. In 1911, continuing reports of success brought about an investigation by Dr. Hugo Munsterberg of Harvard, who allegedly reported favorably on Cayce's strange ability.

In 1912, Edgar ended his partnership with Ketchum and headed to Selma, Alabama, to resume his career in photography. Gertrude and Hugh Lynn followed him to Selma, which was to remain their home for the next eleven years. In 1918, a second son, Edgar Evans, was born. Two years later, Edgar and Hugh Lynn headed for Texas with David Kahn, a Kentuckian they had known for five years, to form the Cayce Petroleum Company. Although Cayce's readings gave frequent hopes of bringing commercial success in the oil prospecting business, within two years the venture failed and he began a national lecture tour giving readings for the public in Columbus, Denver, Birmingham, New York, Pittsburgh, Chicago, Kansas City, and Dayton. The mid-1920s were the most unstable years of Cayce's life and the most pivotal. On September 10, 1923, in Selma, he hired Gladys Davis to be his secretary, and she was to record virtually every reading for the next twenty-two years. But his plan to settle in Selma and devote himself to the readings was soon abandoned at the instigation of Arthur Lammers.

By 1923, Cayce had been giving medical readings for twenty-two years; he died twenty-two years later. At the precise midpoint of his career as a clairvoyant reader, he went through a transformation that clearly defines his life as before and after Lammers. Arthur Lammers, a prosperous printer from Dayton, had met Cayce during his lecture tour and received a reading.[9] Lammers, a student of Theosophy, decided that the readings could be of interest for reasons other than medical concerns.[10] In his biography of Cayce, Thomas Sugrue summarizes the obsessions that drew Lammers to the seer:

> [W]hat were the mechanics of the subconscious, what was the difference between spirit and soul, what were the reasons for personality and talent? He mentioned such things as the mystery religions of Egypt and Greece, the medieval alchemists, the mystics of Tibet, yoga, Madame Blavatsky and theosophy, the Great White Brotherhood, the Etheric World. Edgar was dazed.[11]

But if the conscious Cayce was bewildered by such talk, in trance he was quite ready to answer any question Lammers could pose. After twenty-two years focusing on one specific talent, Edgar Cayce's clairvoyance was to blossom into the most thoroughly documented case of psychic perception in history, thanks to the catalyst of Lammers's questions. The printer was so fascinated by Cayce that he pursued him to Selma, obtained more readings on arcane subjects, and persuaded him to come to Dayton alone to investigate esoteric astrology. In a reading on astrology recorded by Lammers's business associate Linden Shroyer, Cayce spontaneously volunteered the comment that Lammers "once was a monk." Reincarnation, a doctrine alien to the waking Cayce, was an integral part of the cosmic evolutionary scheme outlined in his readings in Dayton.[12] Cayce's immediate reaction was anxiety about the incompatibility of the doctrine with his Biblical faith.

Cayce's chosen biographer was unaware, however, that Lammers was not his first point of contact with Theosophy. A year earlier, in October 1922, the *Birmingham Age-Herald* had reported on a lecture he gave to the Birmingham Theosophical Society. Although he spoke entirely on his healing work, this exposure to the Theosophical milieu provided at least minimal familiarity with the organization that had played a crucial role in preparing the ground for reception of Cayce's readings. Lammers was not the first person to bring astrology to Cayce's attention, either, as is seen in readings on the subject from as early as 1919.

Although Cayce's association with Lammers was short-lived, ended by financial crises in the printer's career, it is recognized by contemporary A.R.E. publications as the crucial turning point in his life. Mark Thurston and Christopher Fazel write, "The entire legacy of his spiritual information can be traced to that insignificant request made by a single passing character."[13] While living in Dayton, Cayce came to the attention of another man whose influence on his life was to be more sustained. Morton Blumenthal, a native of Altoona, Pennsylvania, was a young financier rapidly becoming a millionaire on Wall Street. He was also an explorer of spiritual philosophy, dreams, and the writings of Ouspensky and Blavatsky. For the next seven years, the support of Blumenthal and his brother Edwin was to virtually dominate the Cayce family's existence. The readings had indicated for some time that Virginia Beach was the most auspicious location for Cayce's work to unfold. Blumenthal provided the financial support for the family to relocate there, with the goal of opening a hospital where the readings could be applied by qualified medical personnel. In May 1927, an organization dominated by Blumenthal, the Association of National Investigators, was founded to promote and explore Cayce's work. Eighteen months later, the Cayce Hospital opened in Virginia Beach. Cayce's cousin Dr. Thomas House came from Kentucky to direct the hospital. But while the Cayce Hospital was successful in attracting patients and made a promising beginning, a succession of blows fell upon the work, necessitating a complete change of direction for Cayce by 1931. Dr. House died in October 1929 and three months later an osteopath, Dr. Lydic, became the new hospital director. In the fall of 1930, Atlantic University opened with Hugh Lynn's former psychology professor at Washington and Lee University, Dr. William M. Brown, as president. In the same year a magazine, *The New Tomorrow,* was established. But tensions between Blumenthal and Brown among others came to a head quickly, and the hospital became Blumenthal's sole property in September. By February 1931, under the effects of the Depression, patient frustration with the long-term nature of treatment, and continued conflict, the hospital closed and the Association was disbanded.

1931 marked both an all-time low for Cayce and the beginning of a whole new life. On June 6, a group of supporters met with the Cayces to form a new organization, the Association for Research and Enlightenment, incorporated the following month. On September 14, the first A.R.E. Study Group formed, studying readings that eventually developed into the Search for God books, which continue to be texts for thousands of Study Group members around the world. In the same year, however, the Cayces were obliged to leave the home Blumenthal had provided them, and on a trip to New York in the fall, Edgar was arrested on a fortune-telling charge.

He had been set up by two New York policewomen, pretending to seek readings and possibly inspired by Blumenthal. Front-page photographs of Edgar with Gladys Davis were accompanied by jeering headlines. But the judge dismissed the charges, finding the readings to be psychical research by a bona fide organization devoted to that purpose. In 1932, Atlantic University was forced to close due to continuing financial constraints; it did not reopen until the 1980s. This period of outward discouragement was also marked by the continued outpourings of Study Group readings, soon supplemented by readings for a healing prayer group. During the remaining years of Cayce's life, the Association gradually developed and increasing attention was attracted to his work. 1935 brought another arrest, this time in Detroit, where a reading was given for a child whose father disapproved of Cayce's work and took the reading to a doctor who pronounced the recommended treatment worthless. The father then filed charges with the police. The Cayce family was arrested for practicing medicine without a license, but charges were dropped against all but Edgar. Although he was convicted, the judge imposed no fine or sentence.[14]

For the final decade of his life, Cayce enjoyed the stability and support that had until then been so elusive. The family remained in a home on Arctic Crescent in Virginia Beach, where Cayce devoted his leisure hours to gardening and fishing. The growth of the Association made it necessary to add an office to the Cayce residence in 1940. Two years later, Norfolk Study Group #1 published *A Search for God*, based on the Study Group readings and their years of applying the lessons. In March 1943, Thomas Sugrue's highly sympathetic biography *There is a River* was published to wide acclaim, producing a huge demand for readings. An article calling Cayce the "Miracle Man of Virginia

Beach" appeared in *Coronet* six months later, further increasing the workload. Despite being warned by the readings themselves that no more than five readings per day could be done without serious risk to his health, Cayce yielded to the public demand, exacerbated by wartime worries, by increasing his workload to eight readings per day. After maintaining this schedule for a year, Cayce fell victim to a stroke in September 1944 and went away to Roanoke, Virginia, for a rest. Against the advice of doctors, he returned home to Virginia Beach, where he died on January 3, 1945. Less than three months later, on April 1, Gertrude died of cancer. Hugh Lynn and Edgar Evans were both serving in the military at the time, but the Association had built up a core of knowledgeable workers such as Gladys Davis, Harmon and June Bro, and Mae Gimbert St. Clair. Due to an unexpected gift, the former hospital building, which had been transformed several times for various uses including a hotel and Masonic lodge, was acquired in 1956 as the Association's headquarters. In 1975, a modern library and conference center was added to the site.[15]

Each decade since Cayce's death has been marked by expanded publicity for his work and growth for the Association. In the 1950s, Gina Cerminara's *Many Mansions* and *The World Within* presented Cayce's teachings on karma and reincarnation to a mass audience. Morey Bernstein's *The Search for Bridey Murphy,* a national best-seller in 1956, also devoted attention to Cayce, and a new biography by Joseph Millard, *Edgar Cayce: Mystery Man of Miracles,* further increased public awareness of the readings. In 1967, Jess Stearn's *Edgar Cayce: the Sleeping Prophet* spent six months on national best-seller lists, and the A.R.E. inaugurated a highly popular paperback series of studies of different aspects of the readings, starting with *Edgar Cayce on Reincarnation* by Noel Langley.[16]

A.R.E. membership, which was 3,300 in the mid-sixties, is now approximately 30,000. The most widely read author of the 1970s in the occult/New Age genre, Ruth Montgomery, has testified repeatedly to her appreciation of Cayce. In the 1980s, Shirley MacLaine again focused public attention on him, helping to popularize "channeling," a term found in the readings. Cayce's centrality to the New Age movement continues to be seen in the 1990s, as best-selling author Dannion Brinkley lectures to thousands annually and endorses the Cayce philosophy.

Scholarly investigation of the Cayce phenomenon, however, has lagged far behind the interest shown by popular culture. As the date Cayce set for the Aquarian Age (1998) arrives, it seems an appropriate time to turn to his readings with objective but sympathetic scholarship, examining them in cultural context and evaluating them in historical terms. Andrew Weeks, biographer of Jacob Boehme, defines a pivotal figure as "one into whom all the earlier currents flowed and out of whom these currents spread after being transformed by the force of his inspiration."[17] The readings of Edgar Cayce are a pivotal transformation from the "ancient wisdom" of the nineteenth-century occult revival to the holistic, therapeutic approach of the contemporary New Age movement. His legacy is so complex and yet-unexplored as to be a virtual treasure trove for scholars of religious history.

It is hoped that the present study will be followed by many scholarly works exploring various aspects of Edgar Cayce. This book attempts to place him in context in two ways. First is the historical context of his ideas. This involves comparing and contrasting them with those of his contemporaries, and tracing their precursors in previous literature. Second is the critical context of scientific and scholarly perspectives on the subjects he discusses, which receives almost equal attention.

Cayce's paranormal ability has been most attested in reference to his medical readings. Chapter 1 traces the general health guidelines in the readings and their relationship to the holistic health movement. This is followed by a description of the skeptical literature questioning the value of Cayce's medical readings, contrasting it with research supporting their efficacy. Chapter 1 concludes with an examination of Cayce's approach to health in context of the transition from the metaphysical healing movements New Thought, Unity, and Christian Science to the contemporary New Age and holistic health movements.

Although steeped in Biblical language and symbolism, the Cayce readings interpret Jesus Christ differently than does traditional Christianity. His identification of the Christ principle with a universal Higher Self present in all humanity echoes previous Gnostic, esoteric, and theosophical interpretations. This approach is pivotal in the emergence of a New Age current in Christianity. Chapter 2 explores Cayce's Christology with emphasis on its Theosophical character.

Cayce's "life readings" traced the past lives of subjects, with particular emphasis on Atlantis, ancient Egypt, and Palestine at the time of Jesus. The portrayal of history in such readings is examined in chapter 3, in light of similar material from esoteric literature. Cayce's dramatic prophecies of future events include the beginning of the New Age in 1998. Many of his predictions have failed dramatically, but others have been confirmed in surprising detail. Chapter 3 concludes with a discussion of Cayce's abilities as a reader of the past and future, and explores his own explanations of their limitations.

Chapter 4 explores Cayce's role as a spiritual psychologist. A large share of the Cayce readings for individuals focus on attitudes and emotions, which are discussed in the readings in ways that cohere surprisingly well with current knowledge. His paradigm of the nature of human consciousness and psychic phenomena is reminiscent of Blavatskian Theosophy. Therapeutic emphases in the readings are similar to Jungian psychology, especially in dream interpretation, as well as the Fourth Way teachings of Gurdjieff and Ouspensky. Cayce's astrological readings focus almost entirely on the planets rather than signs and houses, tying astrology to reincarnation in an unusual synthesis. Meditation techniques taught in the readings parallel surat shabd yoga as taught in the Radhasoami movement. After examining all these connections, chapter 4 concludes with a discussion of alternative explanations of how material from published and unpublished texts found its way into the readings.

Evaluation of truth and fiction in the readings is an ongoing process, with varying methodologies depending on the subject matter. Chapters 1 and 3 discuss areas in which truth is empirically accessible. Comparing Cayce's medical readings with the scientific and therapeutic information that has become available since his death, one can evaluate them by an objective, if not infallible standard. His claims about history and the future can be checked, respectively, for correspondence to scholarly reconstruction of the past and recorded events after his death. But in matters spiritual and psychological the ground on which the inquirer stands is far less solid. The most fruitful question then becomes less "Is the material in the readings true or false?" and more "With whose truths do Cayce's cohere?" In the more objective domains of Cayce's clairvoyance, fiction can be identified as incorrect information that appears in the readings. But in the subjective realm of the spiritual advisor, fiction may be the vehicle for the communication of deeper truths.

Introducing scholars to the Cayce readings, this book summarizes their major themes and the issues they raise, as well as their relationship to previous literary sources. Introducing Cayce's admirers to scholarly questions about the readings, it examines the credibility of various aspects of his work in light of current historical and scientific understanding. As a general work, the book addresses many questions briefly which merit detailed investigation in more specialized studies. I offer it in hopes that scholarly investigation of the readings, both within and without the A.R.E., will be stimulated by this preliminary effort.

1.1

Edgar Cayce, circa 1910.

1

Holistic Health Advisor

Edgar Cayce understood his psychic gift primarily in medical terms for the first half of his forty-four-year history as a clairvoyant reader. Even after the life, work, and Study Group readings had unfolded a rich and complex body of doctrines, medical readings retained priority for Cayce. Any attempt to evaluate him fairly must begin with a consideration of their value, the influences that can be discerned in them, and the evidence they offer for and against Cayce's clairvoyance.

Cayce is often called the father of the holistic health movement, and not only in A.R.E. literature. This might be considered an excessive claim, since Cayce tapped into existing trends in health care rather than creating completely new treatments. On the other hand, his medical readings provide more than just a hodgepodge of treatment modalities, indeed offering a consistent approach. This approach to health coheres with that of the contemporary New Age movement, and increasingly with medical practice as well. If not its father, Cayce is at least one of the major forerunners of the holistic health movement.

An essential holistic theme in the readings is conveyed in the message that "The body—physically, mentally, spiritually—is one *body,* yet in the varied conditions as arise within a physical body, these must often be treated as a unit—that is, each element treated as a unit yet in the fullest application they are *one.*"[1] More than two-thirds of the Cayce readings primarily concern the physical body, but even these medical readings are replete with reminders that the physical is an outward expression of what the mind has built.

The Medical Readings

Despite variation among different cases of the same disease, and specific instructions relevant only to particular ailments, there is a high degree of consistency in Cayce's approach to illness. Regardless of the presenting condition, most readings include similar guidelines. For example, headaches were attributed to digestive disorders, and sufferers were advised to adopt a diet of fresh vegetables and fruits, supplemented by fish, fowl, and lamb, avoiding "white bread, combinations of starches, fried foods, sugar, red meat, and carbonated drinks."[2] This is virtually the same diet advice given for everyone. Spinal manipulations, electrotherapy, and hydrotherapy were often suggested. Colonics, enemas, and laxatives were frequently part of the treatment proposed. Castor oil packs and massage were suggested in many cases for a great variety of conditions, and constitute the apparent bedrock of Cayce's health care system. Specific conditions received relevant recommendations, e.g., inhalation therapy for influenza, support hose for varicose veins, surgery for tonsillitis, and ointments for hemorrhoids. Cayce treatments combined most widely accepted practices of medical doctors with some highly unorthodox methods. Among electrotherapy sources were the Wet Cell Appliance, "a galvanic battery that produces a small but measurable electric current" that Cayce believed "stimulated the growth of nerve tissue and connections between nerve tissues" and recommended in about 975 readings.[3] Slightly fewer readings suggested use of the Violet Ray, a high-frequency device providing diathermy, "therapeutic heating of tissues beneath the skin."[4] A particularly strong emphasis on proper elimination is found in frequent suggestions of colonics, enemas, and laxatives, but also of external hydrotherapy, believed "to stimulate the perspiratory system to eliminate toxins through the pores of the skin."[5] This included steam baths, whirlpool baths, and cabinet sweats. Among the reasons given for massage was the belief that it promoted the same kind of elimination. Cayce's pharmacology includes many substances prescribed in the readings, of which the most commonly mentioned are atomidine, a form of iodine described as beneficial to gland functioning, and glyco-thymoline, an antiseptic mouthwash used in many other ways in the readings.

The foundation of the Cayce approach to holistic health is the dietary guidelines given in the readings. For breakfast, one should have cereals or citrus fruit juices, but never combined; fruit, whole wheat bread, eggs, and milk are also suggested. One should lunch on raw salads or vegetable juices, but never with a vinegar-based salad dressing. Cooked leafy vegetables or legumes, with fish, fowl, or lamb in lesser quantity, were the suggested dinner menu.[6] The rationale for the diet is that one should "Keep those foods that are the more alkaline; that is, do not take red meats . . . no fried foods."[7] Acetic acid is to be avoided, as are various food combinations, such as starches and sweets, citrus juices and milk or cereal, multiple starches, oysters and whiskey, coffee and milk or cream, or tomatoes and meats.[8] Carbonated drinks are strongly condemned, as the "gases . . . are detrimental."[9] Dark breads are said to be preferable to white.[10] The readings advise a ratio of three above-ground vegetables to every root vegetable consumed, and one leafy vegetable to every pod vegetable.[11] Apples are said to be better cooked than raw.[12] Honey should be the preferred sweetener, and refined cane sugar is declared especially harmful.[13] Red wine is recommended, if accompanied by dark bread: "This may be taken between meals, or as a meal; but not too much—and just once a day. Red wine only."[14] Beer and liquor are not recommended, and white wines are advised only with meals. The recommendation of red wine seems prescient in light of recent testimony to its medical benefits. "The French paradox," the low heart disease rate of the French despite their high-fat diet, has been attributed in the popular press to their red wine consumption. Another suggestion that seems ahead of its time is avoidance of "benzoate or any preservative."[15] Aluminum in cooking utensils is discouraged, as "in most people it gradually builds something not compatible with the better conditions in the body-forces."[16]

Some of the Cayce advice regarding diet is identical to the "Hay system" taught by physician William Howard Hay in books published in the 1930s. The division between acid- and alkaline-forming foods, the centrality of vegetables and fruits in the diet, the harmfulness of refined and processed flour and sugar, and the avoidance of certain food combinations are all characteristic of the Hay system as well as Cayce's.[17] The specific combinations to be avoided differ in the two systems, and Cayce's dietary suggestions predate Hay's first publication by several years. All that can deduced from the parallel to the Hay diet is that acid/alkaline balance and food combinations were "in the air" of alternative health literature during Cayce's career. Parallels to other aspects of the Cayce diet can be found in a wide variety of more recent sources, including the American Heart Association.

Growing one's own produce is strongly recommended by Cayce, as is land ownership: "Every individual should own sufficient of the earth to be self-sustaining. For the earth is the mother of all, just as God is the father in the spiritual, the earth is the mother in the material."[18] Apart from the spiritual or psychological benefits of closeness to land, however, is the readings' concern about freshness of produce. They advise, "Do not have large quantities of any fruits, vegetables, meats that are not grown in or come to the area where the body is at the time . . . "[19] Vitamins are recognized as essential, and are defined as "The Creative Forces working with body-energies for the renewing of the body."[20] But vitamin supplements are more beneficial if not taken daily, as constant dosages allegedly interfere with the body's ability to derive vitamins from food.[21] Much of the dietary advice in the readings is in accord with generally accepted standards, more so now than when Cayce gave it. Only recently have the dangers of fats and red meat, or the value of fresh leafy vegetables and moderate wine drinking, been widely recognized. Another reasonable suggestion in the readings is to avoid raw milk due to infection dangers, consuming only dried or pasteurized milk.[22] Perhaps more evident from the standpoint of taste than health is the comment that canned tomatoes are often preferable to "fresh," since the quality of the latter is so unpredictable.[23] Nevertheless, many of the Cayce dietary guidelines are unproven and implausible, for example his claims that "Those who would eat two to three almonds each day need never fear cancer."[24] Although there are sound arguments for minimizing pork consumption, Cayce's reasoning falls short of scientific: "Can anyone fill his body with swine and not eventually become piggish or hoggish in his relationships with others?"[25] (Elsewhere, the difficulty of digesting pork is cited, so this passage may not be entirely serious in nature; jokes are not unknown in the readings.) Just as peculiar is the comment that "One leaf of lettuce will destroy a thousand worms," which refers to pinworms.[26] The readings suggest a three-day raw apple diet for cleansing the digestive system, and gave one cancer patient a watermelon diet.[27] But despite some oddities like these, and the forbidden food combinations, the general dietary advice given by Cayce has been solidly confirmed in the half century since his death.

Regular exercise is strongly encouraged in the readings, which call walking outdoors the best exercise.[28] The upper body should be exercised in the morning, the lower in the evening, for "equalizing the circulation."[29] Massage is frequently recommended as a followup to exercise. Stretching in the morning is strongly encouraged. Cayce insisted on balance between work and play, and the importance of esthetic pursuits: "Keep thine body fit. Keep thine mind attuned to beauty . . ."[30]

Favorable Evidence

One of the more unusual aspects of Cayce's medical clairvoyance is its recognition by physicians with whom he worked. Cayce's initial partnership with Al Layne, an unlicensed osteopath, was crucial to the direction his life took after the turn of the century. A few years later, Wesley Ketchum's "discovery" of Cayce brought nationwide attention to his gifts as a result of reports to his homeopathic colleagues. Readings frequently required cooperating doctors in order to implement the treatments proposed. Five years after Cayce's death, journalist Sherwood Eddy conducted a survey of eleven doctors who had cooperated with the readings. Two had handled too few cases to participate, but the remaining nine gave answers that were consistently favorable about the accuracy of diagnosis and the efficacy of treatments prescribed. A doctor in Bronxville, New York, evaluated Cayce's diagnoses as 100 percent correct in the twelve cases he had treated. After treating more than twenty persons who had received readings, a Detroit physician estimated the accuracy of diagnosis at eighty to ninety percent. A Washington physician who had seen five patients with Cayce readings gave an eighty percent accuracy rating to the diagnoses. In Albany, New York, a cooperating physician stated that all five patients he had seen had received correct diagnoses. Of nine cases seen by a Port Washington, New York, doctor, the medical readings were correct in diagnoses for all but one. A New York physician who had treated 100 patients with readings by Cayce estimated the accuracy of diagnosis as eighty percent. Another gave no statistical estimates but said that Cayce's diagnoses were "very good." The closest to a dissenting voice was from a Norfolk, Virginia, doctor who said Cayce's diagnoses could not be considered scientific, but still gave evidence of "extraordinary powers."[31] The consensus among the respondents was that Cayce's diagnostic accuracy compared favorably to that of other physicians, but was by no means perfect. The efficacy of his treatments was rated just as favorably as the diagnoses. The Norfolk physician concluded that "a fair share of those who have been inspired and strengthened to a sincere effort have profited," although "Others lacking in will power and self-discipline have not."[32] The Bronxville doctor estimated ninety percent cured; his Detroit and Washington colleagues gave estimates of eighty and seventy percent respectively. The survey question asked about "cures or improvement," and some of the respondents did not speak specifically of complete cures. A Hopkinsville physician said that all the cases showed improvement, as did the Port Washington doctor, who added that some results were "nothing short of miraculous and a source of consternation to local physicians."[33] The Albany respondent reported "marked improvement in all cases," while the second Washington doctor said that in all cases he "was able to get results."[34] Eddy's last question was "Have you been impressed with anything unique or significant in these cases of Mr. Cayce? Do you believe that there is a 'supernormal' element in his work?"[35] All nine answered affirmatively.

Objections to this survey can be anticipated. First, Eddy does not specify what kinds of physicians reported; the word of naturopaths, chiropractors, and osteopaths carries much less weight with skeptics than that of allopathic practitioners. Even so, Cayce remains unusual among trance psychics in his cooperative relationships with physicians, and in the consistently favorable testimony to his powers found in their reports. Another objection is the small size of Eddy's group of respondents, and their self-selection. Only doctors already adhering to the "Cayce cult," it might be argued, would cooperate with the readings in the first place. Nevertheless, the tone of their responses does not in most cases indicate fervent belief in Cayce, but rather bemused admiration. Sherwood Eddy had obtained a reading for himself in 1938, after hearing five New York physicians testify to the efficacy of the readings. One of the doctors, a personal friend of Eddy, had sought a reading for his own hemorrhages, and was fully cured within a few weeks of beginning the prescribed treatment.[36]

The most prolific author on the medical aspect of the Cayce work is William A. McGarey, M.D., formerly director of the Edgar Cayce Foundation Medical Research Division. Inspired by Hugh Lynn Cayce's urgings that the Cayce medical readings receive study by competent physicians, McGarey and his wife Gladys, also an M.D., established the A.R.E. Clinic in Phoenix, Arizona, in 1970. This followed fifteen years of study of the readings by McGarey, who according to Jess Stearn, "began treating difficult cases with castor oil packs and other Cayce remedies" in 1957, and was amazed at their success.[37] Beginning with the McGareys and a few aides, the Clinic had grown by 1983 to a staff of forty.[38] Subsequently the McGareys divorced; Gladys now heads a Scottsdale, Arizona, clinic also applying the Cayce readings. William McGarey identifies Cayce's approach as holistic, pointing out areas in which the readings are particularly relevant to the emergence of a holistic health movement. He describes Cayce's emphasis on "incoordination" as a cause of illness as a "cornerstone in understanding."[39] McGarey portrays Cayce's understanding of the role of the lymph glands and the thymus in the immune system as ahead of his time. Cayce's references to Peyer's patches, lymph tissue found in the intestines, also seem to foreshadow later discoveries of their function.[40] Another aspect in which Cayce was ahead of his time is in appreciating the value of visualization for health.[41] Cayce's use of the term "stress" and his discussion of its effects also was ahead of his time. Spinal manipulation is now more recognized by mainstream medicine than during Cayce's lifetime. Only in recent years is the therapeutic value of massage being widely appreciated in the medical field; massage is the most frequently suggested form of therapy in the readings, according to McGarey.[42] The A.R.E. Clinic in Phoenix utilizes "biofeedback, acupuncture, massage and hydrotherapy, counseling, music, movement and color therapy, osteopathy, diet, meditation, dream study, laying-on-of-hands healing, and therapies from the Cayce readings."[43] Castor oil packs are a peculiar emphasis in the readings, said to stimulate the elimination of poisons from the system through increasing lymph activity.[44] Their use for a wide variety of ailments was explored in the Clinic and continues as an emphasis of both McGareys.

Jess Stearns, in *Adventures into the Psychic,* reports a Harvard researcher (unnamed) who estimated that Cayce's diagnoses were right 100 percent of the time, but his cures only 50 percent effective.[45] The same book has anecdotes about the success of castor oil packs and baldness treatments, and the literature about Cayce is filled with such testimonials. Six case histories are found in *There is a River;* they are cases of epilepsy, "intestinal fever," arthritis, scleroderma, "general debilitation," and eye injury.[46] All cases were at least partially successful according to correspondence examined by Sugrue.

The only recorded effort to analyze the accuracy of the medical readings is described in Hugh Lynn and Edgar Evans Cayce's book *The Outer Limits of Edgar Cayce's Power.* They found that of 150 randomly chosen readings, seventy-four had no response on file at A.R.E. Some of these may have received positive or negative reports by telephone or verbally, but only those returning questionnaires were counted. Of the seventy-six giving written reports, sixty-five reported favorable results. This provides a rate of 85.5 percent favorable and 14.5 percent unfavorable; which compares well to the success of most physicians.[47] Criticisms of this study are discussed below.

An early case that brought acclaim to Cayce was that of Aimee Dietrich, daughter of the local superintendent of schools. She had been afflicted with up to twenty convulsions daily following an infection at the age of two. Cayce's reading identified a spinal injury sustained the day before her illness began, and advised a series of osteopathic adjustments, which after three weeks of treatment proved efficacious. Aimee was soon restored to the normal state of a five-year-old, although she had previously seemed hopelessly mentally retarded.[48] Due to the prominence of her father, the healing of Aimee Dietrich attracted considerable local attention to Cayce.

The testimony that had the greatest impact on Cayce's reputation, however, came from Wesley Ketchum. Ketchum's paper on Cayce was read before a conference of the American Society of Clinical Research by Henry E. Harrower, M.D., of Chicago. According to the *New*

York Times, it generated an immediate deluge of letters and telegrams to Ketchum. In the paper, Ketchum said of Cayce, "I have used him in about 100 cases, and to date have never known of any error in diagnosis, except in two cases where he described a child in each case by the same name and who resided in the same house as the one wanted. He simply described the wrong person. Now this description, although rather short, is no myth, but a firm reality. . . . The cases I have used him in have, in the main, been the rounds before coming to my attention, and in six important cases which had been diagnosed as strictly surgical he stated that no such condition existed, and outlined treatment which was followed with gratifying results in every case."[49]

Another kind of testimonial found in the Cayce literature concerns the clairvoyance involved in locating doctors and medicines. Sometimes readings gave names and addresses of recommended doctors, although neither Cayce nor the patient was acquainted with them. A related kind of anecdote appears in David Kahn's *My Life with Edgar Cayce.* A medical reading advised use of "black sulphur," but the pharmacist had never heard of it and used regular sulphur instead. A followup reading stated that this had been done, and was the reason the patient was not progressing. A telegram was sent to Cayce asking where black sulphur could be found, and he wired back, "Parke, Davis, Detroit, Michigan." The pharmacist obtained it, newly on the market to his great surprise, and the patient was successfully cured.[50]

Miraculous cures of members of the Cayce family form a part of the anecdotal lore supporting Cayce's abilities. In an article entitled "My Life and Work," Cayce described the first time he used the readings for his own family:

My wife became very ill. After several months under the care of three or four physicians, the one in charge of the case called me to his office one morning and said, "Cayce, I am sorry to tell you, but your wife cannot possibly live another week. Everything possible that I know has been done. One lung is choked. No air has been going through it for months. The other is now affected and you must know from the hemorrhages it is bleeding. With the high temperature, with the little resistance, she can not hold out. I will come whenever she wants me, but if there is anything in this monkey business you are doing you had better try it."

Will anyone ever understand what it meant to me to know that I was taking the life of one near and dear to me in my own hands, and that the very force and power I had been wishy-washy in using for years must now be put to a crucial test?[51]

A reading was duly held, and it said there was hope for Gertrude's recovery. The suggestions in the readings were followed closely, and gradually the patient was restored to health. A few years later, Hugh Lynn was also healed in a way that confirmed the family's faith in Edgar's gift. This healing is described by Edgar:

> Some years ago I had this experience, which came very close to home. An accident happened, and my wife and I didn't feel it was possible for any aid to come to our little son, who was suffering because of an explosion of flash-light powder in his face. The physician told us nothing could possibly be done. Yet when he told us that the child would never see any more, and that his eyes must be taken out if he could even live, the child himself said: "No. 'cause my daddy when he's asleep is the best doctor in the world, and daddy will tell you what to do and you will do it, won't you?"
>   The physician promised that he would follow what the reading said; in fact, he did so, and the boy was healed. Did I do anything? Did the doctor do anything? You ask any physician who saw this happen and they will all tell you just as they did me, "It was just a miracle."[52]

Edgar Cayce's ESP, a small book in the A.R.E. Membership Series by Kevin Todeschi, includes a number of impressive anecdotes from the medical readings and reports. There is no critical scrutiny of Cayce's failures, but the successes are well documented and striking. For example, in one case a reading was given for someone who had called on the telephone while Cayce was in trance; he accurately diagnosed her daughter's injury and identified the locations of both the caller and her daughter. This occurred spontaneously at the end of the scheduled reading, surprising everyone concerned including Harmon Bro, who had been conversing with the caller by phone at the time that Cayce was giving the previous reading in another part of the house.[53] Many such cases are recounted by Todeschi, citing supportive evidence in the form of letters from grateful recipients of readings. But his book presents the evidence that Cayce at times demonstrated clairvoyance, telepathy, and precognition, without exploring the conflicting evidence of his errors.
    In addition to statistical and anecdotal evidence of the readings' accuracy, there are a few topics on which they startlingly foreshadow

discoveries made long after Cayce's death. For example, a reading advised, "Keep the pineal gland operating and you won't grow old—you will always be young!"[54] A best-selling 1995 book, *The Melatonin Miracle*, launched a national explosion of consumption of the hormone. Subtitled *Nature's Age-Reversing, Disease-Fighting, Sex-Enhancing Hormone*, the book reports results of research that support Cayce's claim. Melatonin production by the pineal gland declines with age. The authors conclude that taking it as a dietary supplement will retard aging. The book states that the pineal's function is "to regulate and harmonize the functioning of a number of our bodily systems," including the endocrine and immune systems, and it thereby serves as "the body's aging clock," reporting several studies in support of this conclusion.[55] Another comparably avant-garde bit of Caycean advice is that "The sun during the period between eleven or eleven-thirty and two o'clock carries too *great* a quantity of the actinic [ultraviolet] rays that make for destructive force to the superficial circulation," although moderate sunbathing can be beneficial.[56] Only in recent years has the danger of excessive sunbathing, especially at midday, been fully recognized.

The most scholarly works on the Cayce medical readings are by Eric Mein, M.D., who spend a year in residence at Atlantic University examining them in detail. His 1989 *Keys to Health* analyzes the Cayce approach to health and discusses his treatments for a number of diseases. (Reba Karp's *Edgar Cayce Encyclopedia of Healing* gives detailed reports on all the diseases and treatments discussed in the medical readings.) Mein concludes that "The bottom line on the readings' accuracy and applicability is still not known. They have never been worked with in a systematic manner or had their efficacy closely scrutinized."[57] Recently, plans were announced to build a new facility at A.R.E. headquarters housing a research institute devoted to the medical readings, but Mein's judgment remains valid eight years after his book was written. On the other hand, he finds the medical readings to be consistent, coherent, and insightful on many health issues. Moreover, he concludes that they are more compatible with mainstream medicine than most holistic therapies, and contain many elements that have been confirmed in recent years. For example, Cayce stated that testing a single drop of blood would become the norm for diagnostic purposes, and stressed that the immune system protects against cancer, both of which Mein regards as prescient of contemporary trends.[58] Mein is the founder of the Meridian Institute, which is devoted to research that will "test these [Cayce's] concepts and get them into the mainstream."[59]

Skeptical Critics

Because of the idiosyncratic nature of the readings' medical approach, Cayce has been labeled as a "quack" by some skeptical writers. The first book to attempt to debunk him was by Martin Gardner, whose *In the Name of Science* (1952) was later reprinted as *Fads and Fallacies In the Name of Science* (1957, 1986). Gardner comments that "Sugrue emphasizes the fact that Cayce was a simple, untutored man who could not possibly have possessed the information he gave during his trances, but a far more reasonable supposition is that he absorbed large quantities of knowledge from reading and contacts with friends—knowledge he may have consciously forgotten," alleging further that Cayce "did a vast amount of miscellaneous reading."[60] But no other source supports this allegation, and all the firsthand observers contradict it; in addition to Sugrue, there is the testimony of Hugh Lynn and Edgar Evans Cayce, as well as Harmon Bro, all well-read and well-educated observers, if not impartial ones. No one who knew Cayce is on record as suspecting that he had ever learned by normal means the information he seemed to master in trance.

Gardner admits that "There is no question about the genuineness of Cayce's trances."[61] But he makes the important point that in the early years the trances were given with an osteopath, then with a homeopath, and concludes that "there is abundant evidence that Cayce's early association with osteopaths and homeopaths had a major influence on the character of his readings."[62] In the religious readings, the same could be said of Cayce's association with liberal Protestants, Theosophists, Spiritualists, and New Thought disciples. His vocabulary and concepts clearly reflected those of his environment. Students of Freud, Jung, Ouspensky, and Blavatsky numbered among those who sought readings, and Cayce's psychology reflects all these sources. Gardner's hypothesis is that the readings contain "little bits of information gleaned from here and there in the occult literature, spiced with occasional novelties from Cayce's unconscious."[63] But unless there was a monumentally successful coverup, involving Cayce's entire family and many of his associates, the gleaning of information from occult literature was not carried out primarily by the waking Cayce, but rather in the altered state of consciousness in which he gave the readings. In their book *The Outer Limits of Edgar Cayce's Power,* his sons explain why this conclusion is inescapable for those who knew Cayce personally. If he had conscious access to the information in the readings, they reason, he deliberately and skillfully concealed it for forty-three years, even from those closest to him. This leaves, however, the possibility that he unconsciously fabricated the information in the readings from letters and questions. The authors find this implausible, in light of the frequency of cases in which no information was volunteered by the person seeking the reading. In a random sample of 150 cases from the years 1910–1944, they found thirty-five offering no information prior to the reading. Only forty-six of the 150 were present for the reading; in these cases one might hypothesize that information was somehow derived from them in personal conversation. The authors maintain, however, that Cayce made a point of avoiding conversation with subjects prior to giving a reading. Of forty-two who provided partial information, the authors conclude that thirty-six of the readings contained further information not available to Cayce from previous communications.[64] A fuller examination of this question is presented in chapter 4.

James "the Amazing" Randi savages Edgar Cayce in his *Flim-Flam!* (1987), with special attention to the book by his sons. He opens discussion of the topic by mentioning that "When all else fails to convince the skeptic, promoters of the paranormal fall back on the Sleeping Prophet . . . "[65] Randi complains of "the myriad half-truths, the evasive and garbled language, and the multiple 'outs' that Cayce used in his readings."[66] Here is one skeptic who clearly regards Cayce as a conscious fraud. The tone of Randi's discourse can be discerned in such passages as "Cayce's 'cures' were pretty funny. He just loved to have his patients boiling the most obscure roots and bark to make nasty syrups."[67] Although he makes no effort to appear unbiased, even Randi admits that "the matter is hard to prove, either way" regarding the efficacy of Cayce's cures.[68] He points out quite reasonably, however, that the non-respondents to A.R.E. questionnaires may have all died, or at any rate been dissatisfied, which would drastically reduce the success rate estimated by Hugh Lynn and Edgar Evans.[69] Even when cures were reported, the possibility of spontaneous improvement or placebo effect must be acknowledged. Randi concludes that assuming the non-reports to be negative reduces the positive ratio to only 23.3 percent.[70]

A more balanced and comprehensive critique than those made by Gardner and Randi was published in *The Skeptical Inquirer* in early 1996. The author, Dale Beyerstein, makes many points that merit consideration by Cayce's admirers and detractors. The implicit message of the article, however, is not supported by the evidence and arguments. Beyerstein points out that for the first nine years of the readings, Cayce was always in the presence of a mentor with medical knowledge: first the self-educated osteopath Layne, followed by the medical doctor John Blackburn, and finally the homeopath Wesley Ketchum. (Blackburn was responsible for arranging a meeting in Bowling Green at which several doctors injured Cayce during efforts to find out if he was in a genuine trance.) He concludes that while "it is true that Cayce was not formally trained in any of these professions, he had ample help mastering the jargon."[71] In fact, however, the readings use osteopathic jargon far more than that of homeopathy. Indeed, they state that "As a *system* of treating human ills, osteopathy—*we* would give—is more beneficial than most measures that may be given."[72] Osteopathy is mentioned in 4,733 documents on the CD-ROM, compared to thirty-three for naturopathy and thirty for homeopathy. These figures distort the picture somewhat, however, since Cayce adhered to some naturopathic conventions without calling them by that name. But the basic idea of combining conventional medicine with spinal manipulation, massage, diet, and exercise is a keynote of osteopathic practice. Cayce's wide range of folk remedies provides evidence of fundamental compatibility with the naturopathic approach, as does his aversion to drugs and surgery except in extreme cases.

Beyerstein dismisses the records of the readings preserved in Virginia Beach as "worthless by themselves," objecting that there is no record of information available to Cayce before the readings, or of followup reports.[73] This is a misinformed judgment. The readings themselves are available at the A.R.E. Library in bound volumes with accompanying documents, and a CD-ROM has been available for several years that more than answers Beyerstein's objections. Background correspondence and followup reports are included in full, totaling nearly 100,000 pages, greatly facilitating research. The full text of readings, medical and other, is provided along with precisely the information that Beyerstein claims is unavailable. Statistical analysis of the data is quite feasible, but in light of the author's dismissive comments one wonders if he would consider it worthwhile; he refers to reports from recipients of readings as "anecdotes that are now unverifiable."[74] This implies that they do not merit further investigation, which seems inconsistent with the previous claim that such documentation is unavailable. Beyerstein does, however, make five reasonable points about weaknesses in the evidence for Cayce's medical ability.

First, he points out that corroborating evidence from cooperating physicians "is not independent of what it is taken to confirm," since such physicians were already predisposed to sympathy with Cayce.[75] Corroboration from completely independent sources carries more weight in Cayce's favor than that from confirmed admirers, and is uncommon but not entirely absent from the files. Second, the author observes that no control group studies were ever done to compare the efficacy of Cayce's treatments with placebos. Therefore, "we have no reason to believe that the patient would not have recovered just as well had he or she never heard of Cayce."[76] But even in orthodox medical research, there are areas in which control group studies are rejected as unethical. Although such studies would surely provide stronger confirmation than is now available for the Cayce record, Beyerstein overstates his conclusion. The strength of the evidence varies greatly from case to case, making such a sweeping dismissal unjustified. Corroborating documents in some cases indicate that physicians had diagnosed the patients as incurable. Third, the author points out that patients' memories are unreliable, making their reports less valuable as evidence than actual medical records would be. This point is incontestable, but again the author seems to draw more implications than are justified. Some patients gave reports immediately after their treatment, for conditions that were short-lived (for example problem pregnancies) and therefore not liable to the same possible distortion as reports made about long-term chronic conditions or at a greater distance in time from the events. Fourth, Beyerstein warns that "subjective validation" contaminates the database, in that people were so strongly motivated to believe in Cayce that they would imagine positive results where there were none. It is true that corroboration from medical experts would strengthen the case that any given cure was genuine and guard against the contamination of the data base with subjective validation. Finally, the author warns that some of the "doctors" who corroborated Cayce's cures may have been chiropractors, naturopaths, and homeopaths, as well as poorly trained medical doctors, thus rendering their testimony less persuasive to scientists.

All these arguments present valid warnings about the shortcomings of the evidence available. But their intended implication does not seem to be the need for highly rigorous investigation of the data; instead the attitude seems to be typical of the Committee for the Scientific Investigation of Claims of the Paranormal, the journal's publisher. In his *Parapsychology: The Controversial Science,* Richard S. Broughton describes CSICOP's "vigorous public relations campaign," which markets a "narrow brand of scientific fundamentalism" that dictates "which scientific questions are worth asking and which are not."[77] Beyerstein, like Gardner and Randi, is completely dismissive of the possibility of anything genuinely paranormal about Cayce. The clearest expression of this attitude is found in Randi's words:

> The matter of Edgar Cayce boils down to a vague mass of garbled data, interpreted by true believers who have a very heavy stake in the acceptance of the claims. Put to the test, Cayce is found to be bereft of real powers. His reputation today rests on poor and deceptive reporting of the claims made by him and his followers, and such claims do not stand up to examination.[78]

The author confuses demonstrating a proposition to be unproven with demonstrating its falsity. Although the proofs of Cayce's powers may be less convincing than his admirers have recognized, Randi offers no proof at all that he has put Cayce to the test and found him "bereft of all powers."

There is plenty of material in the medical readings that might be used as ammunition by critics wishing to depict them as ridiculous. For example, longevity was said to be extended by silver and gold properly applied and turtle eggs.[79] Other odd claims are found, for example that the sex of a child depends on the "discharge of the opposite sex."[80] This is explained to mean that male discharges produce female offspring and vice versa. Crude oil massage is alleged to restore hair when the follicles are still alive.[81] Cayce's insistence that the "Lyden gland," (only occasionally called, semi-correctly, the Leydig) is "that center in which the soul is expressive, creative in its nature"[82] strikes the inquirer as particularly odd, since the cells of Leydig are an exclusively masculine feature. (There are parallel features in the ovary, however.) Peculiar elements like these indicate that the Cayce medical readings merit a fair share of skepticism. But to allow their implausible elements to overshadow their benefits would be as mistaken as the opposite. Either case exemplifies "halo effect," in which a faulty generalization is made on the basis of biased observation. If Cayce partisans have overlooked some of the more problematic aspects of the readings, this is balanced by the skeptics' dismissive attitude toward the entire Cayce legacy.

New Thought to New Age

Edgar Cayce played a pivotal role in the transition from New Thought healing to the New Age holistic health movement. Although Cayce has obvious affinities with New Thought, his most striking prototype in American history was a Spiritualist, Andrew Jackson Davis. Davis, the son of a poor shoemaker in upstate New York, was "discovered" in 1843 at the age of seventeen by an amateur mesmerist named Levingston. From their first session it was clear that Davis

demonstrated an unusual degree of susceptibility to trance clairvoyance; on January 1, 1844, the subject made his first "flight through
space" as he later described it. This refers to "traveling clairvoyance"
which Davis soon decided to devote entirely to healing purposes. Like
Cayce, Davis claimed to travel to his patients through hypnotic suggestion, diagnose illnesses, and prescribe treatments. Levingston established "clairvoyant clinics" in Poughkeepsie, N.Y., and Bridgeport,
Connecticut, featuring Davis as psychic diagnostician. But in 1845,
Davis broke with Levingston and established a partnership with the
Rev. William Fishbough; they opened another clairvoyant clinic in New
York City. There he dictated his series of trance lectures which became
the book *The Principles of Nature.* During his twenties, Davis freed
himself from his sponsor and began writing books explaining his
Harmonial Philosophy. He continued to write many books and to
practice clairvoyant medicine for many years until retiring at age 83,
less than a year before his death.[83] David Bell notes that Davis claimed
to have read only one book, although critics have seen influences in
his writings from contemporary sources.[84] The roots of Davis's version
of Spiritualism are defined by Robert Ellwood as an "amalgamation of
the visionary instruction of Emanuel Swedenborg, the Swedish seer,
concerning the life of the soul and other worlds, with the trance-in-
ducing practice of Franz Mesmer, the father of modern hypnotism."[85]
The Spiritualist movement absorbed many of the Mesmerist healers.[85]
Mesmerists taught that there was a mysterious fluid or force responsible for the healings induced by their treatment methods, but com-
missions of inquiry produced mixed results. Mesmer's "animal
magnetism" was championed by Madame Blavatsky among others,
and greatly feared by Mary Baker Eddy. Gradually, it came to be recognized that the patient was responsible for mesmeric healings, rather
than any outer force.[87] The influence of Mesmerism, outside Spiritualist circles, flowed into mainstream hypnosis but also into the New
Thought movement, first called "mental healing."

The first major exponent of mental healing was Phineas P. Quimby
of Belfast, Maine. After some years of experimentation with Mesmerism, Quimby concluded that it was the patient's confidence in the
treatment that produced results, and not the treatment itself. From
1859 through 1866, Quimby put his newly found theory into practice,
promoting his belief that disease was an error of the mind which
could be cured by overcoming the illusion. His office in Portland,
Maine, was visited by students who became major exponents of mental healing: Mary Baker Patterson (later Eddy), Julius and Annetta
Dresser, and Warren Felt Evans. After Quimby's death, mental healing

was dominated by two major approaches: Eddy's Christian Science and New Thought as promoted by the Dressers, Evans, and others. Eddy's authoritarianism drove away some promising Christian Science teachers. Emma Curtis Hopkins was the teacher of Myrtle and Charles Fillmore, founders of the Unity School of Christianity, Ernest Holmes, founder of Religious Science, and the founders of Divine Science. After excommunication by Eddy in 1885, Hopkins had gone on to become the most important influence in New Thought.[88] 170 documents in the Cayce readings and reports refer to Christian Science, 135 to Unity, sixty-six to New Thought, and twenty to Divine Science.

The Cayce medical readings emphasize the importance of mental and emotional influence on the healing process. Mrs. Eddy's Christian Science is the best known expression of the nineteenth-century mental healing movement. But Christian Science, with its outright rejection of medical care, is the most extreme example of the mental healing movement's legacy. New Thought, a diverse collection of groups focused on similar themes of mental healing, is equally part of the background against which Cayce must be understood. His insistence on the role of Christ in the healing process, like his discussion of attitudes and emotions, shows how much common ground his approach shares with the mental healing movement. The readings state that the resurrection of Jesus Christ implies that God gives the power "that may reconstruct, resuscitate, even every atom of a physically sick body . . . even every atom of a sin-sick soul."[89] Cayce seems to echo the anti-medical attitudes of Christian Science in stating that "The Christ Consciousness . . . is the *only* source of healing for a physical or mental body."[90] This similarity is less definite than it appears, however, for another reading explains that all healing is divine:

> All strength, all healing of every nature is the changing of the vibrations from within, the attuning of the divine within the living tissue of a body to the creative energies. This alone is healing. Whether it is accomplished by the use of drugs, the knife or whatnot, it is the attuning of atomic structure of the living force to its spiritual heritage.[91]

In brief, "healing—all healing—comes from within."[92] What is commonly called spiritual or psychic healing works by awakening the emotions so as "to revivify, resuscitate or to change the rotary force or influence of the atomic forces in the activity of the structural portion, or the vital forces of a body . . . to set it again in motion."[93] Although illness is often karmic in nature, and "Karmic influences must ever be met," Christ has "prepared a way that He takes them upon Himself, and as ye trust in Him He shows thee the way . . . "[94]

Cayce often addressed the significance of attitudes and emotions in medical as well as life readings. Although in some respects Cayce echoes the emphases of the New Thought movement, the readings are considerably more psychologically sophisticated. Three hefty volumes of the Library Series are devoted to excerpts on a wide range of emotions and attitudes. In his introduction to the three volumes, Herbert Puryear, a clinical psychologist, summarizes Cayce's approach. Attitudes are essentially mental in nature, orientations toward experience that determine how we interpret it. Cayce emphasizes that we have free will to modify our attitudes, which are constantly shifting although subject to habitual patterns. Emotions, on the other hand, are more physical than mental, "reaction potentials which are stored deeply within the psychic mechanisms of our beings," according to Puryear.[95] Cayce's key phrase "Mind is the builder" applies to the crucial power of attitudes to evoke emotions and thereby affect the body's health. The readings emphasize the role of the endocrine glands in emotional responses. According to Cayce, emotions are rooted in previous Earth lives. Defining and holding to ideals is the recommended way of keeping one's attitudes constructive and healthy. The readings imply that mental attitudes can be changed much more readily than emotional patterns, because they are more conscious and more amenable to self-knowledge. Emotions are reached indirectly through work on attitudes or through purification of the body. Puryear notes that medical readings often began by addressing the need for attitudinal change.[96] Indeed, sometimes this is given paramount importance in improving physical health, for example in this reading: "There is much more to be obtained from the right mental attitude respecting circumstances of either physical, mental, or spiritual than by the use of properties, things or conditions outside of self, unless these are in accord with the attitudes of the body."[97] Fear is regarded as "the root of most of the ills of mankind," and it can be overcome through the ideals of love, faith, and understanding.[98] Self-condemnation is particularly to be avoided, and anger to be controlled.

The New Thought element in Cayce's approach has more in common with that promoted by the Unity School of Christianity than any other denomination. Christian Science and Theosophy are often criticized in the readings, but Unity is always praised. David Bell notes that Divine Science is also consistently regarded with favor by Cayce.[99] Charles Fillmore of Unity taught a form of kundalini yoga based on twelve centers rather than the Caycean seven. His *Twelve Powers of Man* refers to these as "twelve great centers of action, with twelve presiding egos or identities," which govern "the subconscious realms in man."[100] They include the seven centers of Cayce's system and an additional five, but are equated to nerve ganglia rather than glands as in Cayce's system. In a 1925 letter to an inquirer, Cayce commented on the Unity school as well as Theosophy:

> I do not know but very little of any of the people who hold to the tenets of reincarnation. I believe Unity and its teachings, and Theosophy, hold to these principles. As to how far the developments have been with these, I know very little. I certainly have not gotten any of MY beliefs in these from either of these groups. As to the work of Mr. Fillmore, as head of Unity, I'm sure this has done and is doing a wonderful lot of good in the United States. As for Theosophy, of course that is one of the older societies and partakes, as I understand, of a great deal of the religions of the East, and England has been having considerable trouble with Mrs. Besant, the acknowledged head of the society at present, in India.[101]

Although he makes it clear that he wishes neither to endorse nor condemn either organization, Cayce seems to lean in the direction of Unity. As the sole Christian denomination to teach reincarnation, it is the group that seems most compatible with A.R.E. membership. In addition to emphasis on reincarnation, there are several other points of agreement. The readings offer a large number of affirmations for use with meditation; use of affirmations is standard in the New Thought movement. *Lessons in Truth,* a Unity textbook, explains why: "In reality God is forever in process of movement within us, that He may manifest Himself (all-Good) more fully through us. Our affirming, backed by faith, is the link that connects our conscious human need with His power and supply."[102] The readings are much more ambivalent about Christian Science than Unity, although each was recommended at times. By 1944, Cayce was more familiar with Unity than he had been in 1925, as seen in this letter to an inquirer:

> So far as our association or connection with Unity is concerned, I have worked with many of the leaders in that group. We interchange literature and a great deal of their literature will be found among the books in our library. Quite often we have had instances where people have been referred to this as a portion of

their treatment, just as they have been referred to other groups. Some of the most remarkable readings have been where the information has suggested that the patient use Christian Science, and one of the most wonderful that I recall through the years, after following a certain line of suggestions, the individual was to read Unity entirely.[103]

Cayce echoes New Thought in his insistence that the Christian life is one of fulfillment rather than self-denial: "Do all in the joyous manner, for *His* gospel is the *glad* gospel, the *joyous* life, the happy life."[104] In a rare public statement, Cayce disavowed any intent to start a new healing cult, but affirmed his wish to draw attention to the healing work of Jesus:

> Mental healing has been a portion of almost every new idea that has been presented to the world in recent years as a new religion. I do not want you to think that I am attempting, in discussing the matter, to found a new sect or ism or to have a following of any kind. What I want is to give a better understanding of the Great Physician, that One who was able to heal by the touch of his hand. I want most of all to awaken in people the consciousness of divine healing that He had so completely developed.[105]

Use of the words "Law of" to refer to spiritual principles is equally common in New Thought literature and the Cayce readings, according to David Bell.[106] While "channel" is found in both New Thought and contemporary sources, the meaning has subtly shifted. In New Thought, the term refers to the possibility of being a channel for the divine, as opposed to channeling entities, which J. Gordon Melton traces to the UFO movement.[107] Cayce's use of the term is in its New Thought context. "New Age" is found in Blavatsky and Bailey, among others, but the specific idea that the end of the twentieth century marks its dawning was first emphasized by Cayce.

Phillip Lucas links the A.R.E. to the New Age movement in his essay on the organization in *America's Alternative Religions*. He points out that in the 1970s, "ARE wedded itself to the burgeoning New Age movement and became one of its major promoters," which was "a natural outgrowth of activities and emphases that had long been staples of the association" since "ARE should be viewed as a significant predecessor to the entire New Age phenomenon."[108] He finds "the New Age's eclectic, pastiche-like approach to spiritual traditions and methods"[109] particularly reminiscent of the A.R.E.'s approach.

According to Lucas, there are four distinguishing characteristics of the New Age movement: "Belief in an imminent planetary spiritual transformation that will occur at the level of human consciousness. . . . An ethic of self-empowerment and self-healing as a prerequisite to the healing of society. . . . A desire to reconcile religion and science in a higher synthesis that enhances the human condition both materially and spiritually. . . . Strong eclecticism in its embrace of healing therapies, spiritual practices, and millennial beliefs."[110] No other organization is more quintessentially New Age, according to this set of criteria, than the A.R.E. The idea of imminent spiritual transformation of human consciousness is linked specifically with the term "New Age" in the Cayce readings, for example "the entity has caught that vision of the NEW Age, the new seeking for the relationships of a Creative Force to the sons of men."[111] As discussed in chapter 3, the year 1998 is particularly highlighted by the readings in this regard. Self-empowerment and self-healing are keynotes of the advice Cayce gave about psychological and physical health, and are portrayed as a prerequisite to societal transformation. Reconciliation of science with religion is implicit in the very nature of the organization founded by Cayce, which relates research and enlightenment in its name and its programs. Eclecticism in healing therapies, spiritual practices, and millennial beliefs has been increasingly characteristic of the A.R.E. for several decades.

J. Gordon Melton regards the contemporary New Age synthesis as a result of the convergence of Spiritualism, Theosophy, astrology, and Eastern religion in the United Kingdom in the 1960s. In the seventies and eighties, the New Age's center of gravity shifted to the United States.[112] Phillip Lucas regards the A.R.E. as having been "saved by the New Age," since the association had grown very slowly until the 1960s, but dramatically expanded thereafter. The budget of A.R.E. grew from $81,000 in 1969 to $3,916,000 in 1981, as membership more than doubled. Since then, conference attendance, book sales, and contributions have been relatively steady, although membership grew throughout the 1980s as a result of aggressive direct mail recruitment and then declined sharply when this approach was abandoned.[113]

Although some aspects of the New Age are now regarded as passé, holistic healing has become mainstream. In his *Guide to Alternative Medicine,* Dr. Isadore Rosenfeld notes five characteristics that distinguish holistic doctors from conventional ones. They regard mind and body as one, focus on prevention and health care rather than treatment of disease, believe that medication is not always necessary for healing, treat the "whole patient rather than any one organ or system," and are more concerned with the impact of diet, exercise, psychological states, "the total environment" on health.[114] Rosenfeld notes that in the 1990s all these characteristics are increasingly common among conventional physicians, and that "the real difference between mainstream doctors and those who formally designate themselves as 'holistic' is that the latter also employ a wide variety of controversial treatment methods, from psychic healing, herbs, and megavitamins to immune therapy, homeopathy, reflexology, and naturopathy."[115] In his book, Rosenfeld evaluates the full array of alternative therapies from the standpoint of a skeptical practitioner of conventional medicine, and finds several especially promising but others to be worthless. Massage, Cayce's most frequently prescribed treatment, is experiencing a boom, with mainstream physicians increasingly willing to refer patients to massage therapists. Rosenfeld regards bodywork in general as one of the more promising alternative treatments. Hydrotherapy and meditation, mainstays of the Cayce approach, are also recommended by Rosenfeld without qualification. Spinal adjustment, although increasingly accepted by mainstream medicine, receives a more modest appraisal, as does aromatherapy, an occasional Cayce prescription. Most of the alternative treatments deemed less than worthwhile by Rosenfeld, like chelation, Ayurveda, homeopathy, foot reflexology, and iridology, are not a significant part of the Cayce treatment spectrum. The one exception to this is colonics, which Cayce esteemed highly but Rosenfeld dismisses.

Even the use of clairvoyance in medical diagnosis is becoming more familiar in the 1990s. Two popular contemporary authors, Barbara Brennan and Caroline Myss, claim to see the human energy field (called "aura" by Cayce) including the chakras, and to use this power for healing. Both train students to perform a new kind of spiritual healing based on this perception. Myss cooperates with trained physicians in the treatment of patients, acting as a "medical intuitive" who perceives the condition of internal organs through a process that seems akin to Cayce's. Best-selling authors like Andrew Weil, Daniel Goleman, and Bernard Siegel promote the development of "mind/body medicine," which integrates the fundamental insights of New Thought into the framework of medical science. A striking indication of the convergence of mainstream and alternative medicine is found in Time/Life's recently published *Medical Advisor*. Subtitled *The Complete Guide to Alternative & Conventional Treatments*, it presents a wide array of choices for hundreds of ailments, from a diverse assortment of treatment modalities. The castor-oil pack, Cayce's invention, is included.

The A.R.E. has taken a cautious approach to alternative medicine, urging people to use the medical readings' advice in consultation
with physicians. (Legal concerns may inform this conservatism.) Its
emphasis on massage and hydrotherapy, both of which are available
at the Virginia Beach headquarters, shows an institutional preference
for the less controversial aspects of Caycean health treatment. There
are many unanswered questions about the efficacy of Cayce's medical
readings for the patients who received them, and only a full-scale
investigation of the evidence can begin to address them adequately.
The genuineness of his medical clairvoyance remains a subject of sharp
debate, as does the existence of extrasensory perception in general.
But regardless of these unresolved issues, it can be said with confidence
that the general health guidelines found in the readings have been
increasingly confirmed in the half-century since Cayce's death. Moreover, the holistic, eclectic approach of the readings is far closer to the
mainstream now than it was during Cayce's lifetime.

2.1

Edgar Cayce, early 1920s.

2

Christian Theosopher

Edgar Cayce was the premier Christian theosopher of the twentieth century in the English-speaking world, measured in terms of cultural
influence and literary output. To call him a theosopher is not necessarily
to identify him with the Theosophical movement founded in the nineteenth century by H. P. Blavatsky. Despite his many links to Blavatsky's
teachings, Cayce belongs to a tradition that predates her by many centuries and has recently attracted long overdue scholarly attention.

The leading academic scholar of esotericism, Antoine Faivre,
characterizes theosophy as a "gnosis that has bearing not only on the
salvific relations the individual maintains with the divine world, but
also on the nature of God Himself, or of divine persons, and on the
natural universe, the origin of that universe, the hidden structures that
constitute it in its actual state, its relationship to mankind, and its final
ends."[1] By this definition, Cayce's readings constitute a quintessentially
theosophical revelation. "Gnosis" is defined by Faivre as a "spiritual
and intellectual activity that can give access to a special mode of knowledge . . . a grasp of fundamental relationships including the least apparent that exist among the various levels of reality . . . "[2] Theosophical
gnosticism is distinguished by its reconciliation of transcendence and
immanence, penetrating not only the depths of being but the heights
of divine wisdom.[3] By aspiring to scale the heavens while honoring
the descent of the divine into earthly life, theosophy integrates the
polarities of involution and evolution.[4]

In a groundbreaking 1994 study, Arthur Versluis calls for a
reawakening to the theosophical dimension in Christianity, which he
traces from pseudo-Dionysius the Areopagite to the German mystics
of the seventeenth through nineteenth centuries. Versluis sees in these
theosophers a "paracletic" dimension of Christianity which connects
them experientially rather than historically. His theosophers attempted
to "reconstitute primordial Christianity—to live in a world where the
miraculous is indeed possible, to realize the timeless in the present
moment."[5] Theosophers are linked by their common "homesickness of
the soul," which orients them to a journey homeward to God.[6]

The highest ideal possible for humanity is, in Cayce's words, to "keep the way that will lead to the closer relationship with God, in Christ-Jesus."[7] This way is pursued "because our mind, the Son, is within us."[8] The Godhead is defined in the readings as "That from which the impulse flows, or returns to. The beginning—the end—of all."[9] Cayce's Christology pervades his cosmology, anthropology, psychology, and even his medical readings. The Christ as a cosmic principle is the first emanation from divinity and "as He moved, souls—portions of himself—came into being."[10] "Son of the First Cause" is one synonym for the Christ used in the readings.[11] Because the Christ is the "firstborn of the Father" in this pre-cosmic sense, He is also the way back to the Father in a mystical sense. Through sinful rebellion, humanity has fallen into material existence and forgetfulness, yet retains its primordial soul-identity with the Christ principle immanent in every person. Matter is not inherently evil, but rather an opportunity for "the attributes of the source of good [to] be manifested" as a way for spirit, separated from its source, to find its way back.[12] All souls must attain consciousness "of being one with the influence that makes for growth."[13] All life is part of a journey from "the impregnation of spirit in matter" to the oneness of individual spirit with its source.[14] The idea of Christ as the universal mind, first creation of God, is reminiscent of Plotinus's doctrine of the Nous as the first emanation of the One. There are no references to Neoplatonism or Plotinus in the readings, however.

The readings consistently use Biblical language with a mystical, theosophical twist. For example, "Christ fulfilled the law by compliance with same, He became the law and thus thy Savior, thy Brother, thy Christ!"[15] The law that was fulfilled by Christ was, in Cayce's cosmology, the law of cosmic evolution that determined the unfolding of life in the universe. As the life force expanded into myriad forms, it fulfilled the inherent dynamic of creation, thus becoming the law. Christ is savior and brother in that each person has immediate access to the Higher Self that remains ever ready to help lead back to union with the original source, or Father in Heaven.

The Christ is also identified in the readings with Adam, for "the Son of man entered the earth as the first man."[16] The readings state that Jesus realized that he was to be the world's savior "when he fell in Eden."[17] The same soul has been reincarnated many times, "Christ in all ages, Jesus in one," who in other lives was Melchizedek, Zend, Ur, Asaph, and Joseph.[18] But in Jesus the primordial Christ principle is most perfectly exemplified, for he "thought it not robbery to make Himself equal with God."[19] Thus, Jesus is a role model for everyone who seeks union with his inner divinity, and his suffering and crucifixion are models for all who "must pass under the rod, even as He—who entered into materiality."[20] Jesus manifested God, Life, or Creative Forces in his ministry as well as his death and resurrection. He is therefore a way-shower and a liberator: "HE is thy KARMA, if ye put thy trust WHOLLY in him."[21]

The readings abound in statements that on the surface seem to support an exclusivistic Christian approach, but on closer inspection can be seen to convey a universalist message, for example, "there is only *one* God, *one* Christ, *one* faith, *one* baptism."[22] Cayce uses the language of the Protestant Sunday School teacher he was in his waking life, insisting that Christ loves each of us individually, cares for our needs, "is mindful of thy petitions, of thy aches, thy pains, thy disappointments, thy sorrows, thy joys, thy exultations."[23] The ideal of the Christ Consciousness is the single most emphatic message of the Cayce readings, permeating every aspect of his world view. It can be personalized enough to satisfy the most orthodox of Christians, or depersonalized enough to be acceptable to non-Christians, whom the readings always treat with inclusive respect. This ability to bridge diverse approaches and stimulate mystical experience in a wide range of readers is one of the crucial elements making Cayce a transitional figure of the contemporary New Age movement. When asked if faith in Buddha or Muhammad was as effective as faith in Jesus Christ in its effect on one's soul, Cayce replied "[H]e that receiveth a prophet in the name of a prophet receives a prophet's reward . . . each in their respective spheres are but stepping-stones to that that may awaken in the individual the knowledge of the Son in their lives."[24] Salvation is not from some external judgment or fate, but "Only from themselves! That is, their individual hell; they dig it with their own desires!"[25] What can save us from ourselves is "naught that man can do," but rather "the mercy of the Father as exemplified in the Son."[26] One of the most commonly repeated assertions in the readings is that the Father "wills that no one should perish,"[27] the essential message of universalist Christianity.

The coming of the kingdom of heaven can be hastened by the efforts of believers, if they will manifest the "love of the Father in the earth."[28] A.R.E. Study Group participation is designed to make church members "nearer Christ-like, thus filling their lives with such love that dogmatic principles (as in some churches) are taboo."[29]

The Farewell Discourses

In dozens of readings, Cayce recommended study of one small section of the Bible which he said contained the essential spiritual message of his own work. The fourteenth through seventeenth chapters of the Gospel of John are known as the "Farewell discourses." This is a core text for "paracletic" Christian theosophy, asserting the interpenetration of the Father, the Son, the Holy Spirit, and the soul of the believer. After Jesus says at the conclusion of chapter 13 that he is going where his disciples cannot follow, he reassures them that this need not deprive them of his presence: "Let not your hearts be troubled; ye believe in God, believe also in me. In my Father's house are many mansions; if it were not so I would have told you. I go to prepare a place for you."[30] When Thomas asks how the disciples could know the way without Jesus to show them, he answers "I am the way, the truth, and the life; no man cometh unto the Father, but by me. If ye had known me, you would have known my Father also: and from henceforth ye know him, and have seen him."[31] Philip then asks to be shown the Father, to which Jesus replies that those who had seen him had seen the Father, for "I am in the Father and the Father in me . . . the Father that dwelleth in me, he doeth the works. . . . He that believeth on me, the works that I do shall he do also; and greater works than these shall he do . . . "[32] Jesus then promises that the Father will send a Counselor, the Spirit of truth, and manifest himself to all who love him and keep his commandments.

Chapter 15 opens with the metaphor of Jesus as the true vine, the Father as the husbandman, and the believer as the branch. "I am the vine, ye are the branches. He that abideth in me, and I in him, the same bringeth forth much fruit, without me ye can do nothing."[32] Disciples are not servants of Christ, but friends, for he has shared all his knowledge of the Father with them. But this friendship will bring persecution; in chapter 16, Jesus develops the theme that terrible hatred will afflict the disciples, but reiterates that the Spirit of truth will be sent to guide them into all truth, closing with the promise that "In the world ye shall have tribulation: but be of good cheer; I have overcome the world."[33] In the seventeenth chapter, Jesus announces that the hour of his sacrifice has come, but that no outward separation can break the bond between him and his friends, which will extend to all they convert after his death.

> Neither pray I for these alone, but for them also which shall believe in me through their word; that they may all be one; as thou, Father, art in me, and I in thee, that they also may be one in us: that the world may believe that thou hast sent me. And the glory which thou gavest me I have given them; that they may be one, even as we are one: I in them and thou in me, that they may be made perfect in one; and that the world may know that thou

hast sent me and hast loved them, as thou hast loved me. Father, I will that they also, whom thou hast given me, be with me where I am, that they may behold my glory, which thou hast given me: for thou hast loved me before the foundation of the world.[34]

Because these discourses are the most-cited New Testament passages in the readings, their doctrinal context may yield some clues about Cayce's theological orientation. The Gospel of John was the last to be written, a fact acknowledged by Cayce in a reading, and it has many distinctive emphases that encourage theosophical interpretation. Use of the term "logos" indicates a similarity to noncanonical Gnostic and Hellenistic texts. John omits several of the more human stories about Jesus found in the synoptics; there is no temptation by Satan, anguish at Gethsemane, or announcement of the coming kingdom. According to D. Moody Smith, John "dramatically shifts the focus of eschatology from the future to the present."[35] This may be one reason for Cayce's fondness for Johannine Christianity, but his insistence on the importance of the Farewell discourses suggests a more specific motivation. The tone and message of this section of the gospel is one of reassurance. Jesus will abide with the disciples after his death, in a manner more intimate than depicted in the synoptics. Matthew, Mark, and Luke include apocalyptic discourses warning of catastrophic events leading to a glorious and public return of Jesus. In their place, John offers an eschatology in which Christ returns privately to the individual Christian through the Holy Spirit or Paraclete. Although the resurrection is for John an unquestioned fact, it can only be proven through the work of the Counselor.

In *The Key to Theosophy*, H. P. Blavatsky interprets the esoteric meaning of the metaphor of the vine as speaking of the relationship between the inner divinity or atman and the personality: "Atma(n) is the Husbandman—the Spiritual Ego or *Buddhi* (Christos) the Vine, while the animal and vital soul, the *personality,* is the 'branch.' "[35] This theosophical method of interpretation seems to accord with Cayce's emphasis that "all of God that any individual may know is already within self."[36] John's eschatology of a present union with the eternal logos accords more with such a doctrine than does the synoptics' portrayal of a future kingdom. The core of Gnostic doctrines, whether Christian, Jewish, or Hellenistic, is the goal of return to the source from which all life emanated. In the readings, Cayce insists that "The soul, then, must return—*will* return—to its Maker."[37] Although Johannine themes predominate in the readings, they also include prophecies which like the synoptics warn of future catastrophe and a physical return of Christ; these are discussed in chapter 3.

The Bible passage next most frequently recommended by Cayce after the Farewell discourses is the thirtieth chapter of *Deuteronomy.* This passage appears near the end of the Pentateuch, and follows two chapters warning of future exile from the Promised Land, which the Jews are now approaching as the death of Moses nears. It is also a farewell discourse, the final address of Moses to his people. In chapter 30, it is promised that if Israel is exiled from the Promised Land, but then repents, the homeland will be restored. The most significant passages in terms of Cayce's religious philosophy (and most often quoted in the readings) are verses 11–16:

> For this commandment which I command thee this day, it is not hidden from thee, neither is it far off. It is not in heaven, that thou shouldest say, Who shall go up for us to heaven, and bring it to us, that we may hear it, and do it? Neither is it beyond the sea, that thou shouldest say, Who shall go over the sea for us, and bring it to us, that we may hear it, and do it? But the word is very nigh unto thee, in thy mouth, and in thy heart, that thou mayest do it. See, I have set before thee this day life and good, and death and evil; In that I command thee this day to love the LORD thy God, to walk in his ways, and to keep his command-ments, and his statutes and his judgments, that thou mayest live and multiply: and the LORD thy God shall bless thee in the land whither thou goest to possess it.[38]

The word that is ever present is the law as given to Moses.[39] But Cayce, by constantly pairing this passage with the Farewell discourses, associates the word with the Johannine logos. Thus, the specific prom-ise to the Jews is universalized into a promise to all humanity that the Word shall be ever present within each person. Another frequently stressed implication is that the choice between good and evil confronts us daily, and thus that it is always possible to align oneself with the divine will.

In his meditation instructions, Cayce advised thinking of the "white light of the Christ" not as a color or vibration but rather as "awareness of entering into the spirit of truth, the power of health, the power of love."[40] Although Cayce reiterates the seemingly exclusive claim that "there be no name under heaven whereby men may be saved than in His name!" this is interpreted as meaning that "self's own I AM with the spirit of truth and life, has made aware within self that thou hast been called by name."[41] The call from within comes from the Christ, for "the desire of the soul for harmony and peace is born of Him that gave, 'My peace I give unto thee'; not as the *world* gives peace, but as the *spirit* that makes alive that which gives the knowledge of *His* peace—that peace that passeth all understanding!"[42]

Cayce and the Theosophists

Edgar Cayce was a modern theosopher by the definitions found in the writings of Faivre and Versluis. In an altered state of consciousness, he attained a special mode of knowledge which purported to grasp the fundamental relationships among layers of reality. Through this gnosis, he claimed insight into the nature of God, the spiritual world, and the natural universe. Inspired by homesickness of the soul, Cayce attempted to reconstitute primordial Christianity and recapture the sense of the timeless and the miraculous that the church had seemingly lost. Although his status as a modern theosopher is beyond question, his relationship to the modern Theosophical movement is convoluted and mysterious. Belonging to the metahistorical lineage of Christian mystics whose insights are theosophical in the general sense, Cayce often disagreed sharply with the Theosophy of Madame Blavatsky and her successors. Cayce's spiritual psychology resonates in many ways to Blavatsky's, and his version of esoteric history accords with hers more than any other. But on the central role of Christ as Master, Cayce parts company with Blavatskian Theosophy emphatically and consistently.

When asked in 1933 if the study of any particular part of Blavatsky's *The Secret Doctrine* would be beneficial, he replied that study of any part of the book was valuable, but "only in so far as it will enable the self to open for that which may be given in its meditation."[43] Cayce frequently acknowledged the existence of adepts or Masters, but their significance in his view falls well short of Theosophical idealization of them:

> those of any cult, or any group of people who by constant intro-spection through entering into the silence, are *able to bring* to the surface the activities of the entity as a whole . . . are called sages, lamas, or such. These, when they are *made* to be what is *commonly* termed *practical,* yet remaining spiritual in *aspect* (that is, sticking to the truth!), they become masters. When they are turned to channels that are to *induce* influences over individuals because they have that ability to *hold* an individual, then they *abuse.*[44]

Implicit in this remark appears to be a criticism of the way that some seekers were enthralled by particular masters. Cayce seems to have been surrounded from 1924 on by people familiar with Blavatskian Theosophy. In a dream interpretation for Morton Blumenthal, he referred to various phases of life including the "material, mental, moral, philosophical, theosophical, metaphysical . . . "[45] In 1925, advising Blumenthal about his literary career, Cayce said "In theosophy, theology, approach such periodicals as carry such," naming among others "such as are published by The Theosophical Society."[46] Later in the same year, Blumenthal reported three dreams about Blavatsky's *Isis Unveiled,* which Cayce interpreted to mean that the subject of reincarnation (about which Blumenthal was reading when he fell asleep) required further investigation.[47] Later he again referred to "theology, theosophy," and other issues as being Blumenthal's concerns.[48] (William James, Thomson Jay Hudson, Gurdjieff, and Ouspensky were among Blumenthal's other literary enthusiasms.)[49] In 1942, Thomas Sugrue described the A.R.E.'s membership as drawn from "all of the Protestant churches; from the Roman, Greek, Syrian, and Armenian Catholic churches; from the ranks of Theosophy, Christian Science and Spiritualism; and from many of the Oriental religions."[50] It is not surprising that after the orthodox Christian groups, Theosophy is listed first; it seems to be quite well represented in those who sought Cayce's counsel and is mentioned in fifty readings. Theosophical influence in the minds of A.R.E. members can be inferred from an interrogation of the entranced Cayce by the Executive Committee of Group 9, which seemed insistent on linking Cayce to the Great White Brotherhood. They asked him in 1935 to what extent the Masters of this lodge directed his activities, and which Masters were directly in charge, to which he replied, "Messengers from the higher forces that may manifest from the Throne of grace itself."[51] Unsatisfied with this response, they pressed for specific identifications, asking if Saint-Germain was involved. (The Comte de Saint-Germain was claimed as an adept sponsor not only by Theosophists, but also by Rosicrucians and the newly created I AM movement.) Cayce interrupted, saying "Those that are directed by the Lord of lords, the King of Kings, Him that came that ye might be one with the Father."[52] Again, he was asked if Saint-Germain was among this group, and for the identity of Halaliel, a being that had spoken through him recently. He replied, "These are all but messengers of the Most High," and explained that Halaliel was one of the leaders of the heavenly host. The Saint-Germain question was posed yet a third time, and at last Cayce replied, "When needed." A sense of increasing impatience with this line of questioning is conveyed by the next reply, to the request "Please give us Thine identity." The source indignantly replied, "He that seeks that has not gained the control seeks damnation to his own soul! Control thine inner self that ye may know the true life and light! for he that would name the Name must have become perfect in himself!"[53] The next question continued to insist that the source explain itself in Theosophical terms: "If Mr. Cayce is a member and a messenger of the Great White Brotherhood, how do the Masters wish him to proceed and should not his activities henceforth be presented as Their Work?" To which Cayce responded with even greater clarity:

> As the work of the *Master* of masters, that may be presented when in those lines, those accords necessary through the White Brotherhood. This—this—*this*, my friends, even but limits; while in Him is the Whole. Would thou make of thyself, of thyselves, a limited means of activity? Would thou seek to be hindered by those things that have made of many contending forces that continue to war one with another even in the air, even in the elemental forces? For He, thy Lord, thy God, hath called thee by name, even as He has given, "Whosoever will drink the cup, even as of my blood, he may indeed be free."[54]

Despite the obvious rebuke in the above passage, the inquirers continued their questioning, asking whether a Foundation for the work of the Masters should be established by Cayce and his supporters. In his reply, he alluded once again to Jesus Christ: "As to foundations, as to locations, as to sites, how gave he? 'Neither in this mountain nor yet in Jerusalem, but rather in the hearts,' the lives, the souls of those who have named the Name and put *on* Him that is the Way!"[55]

In 1933, a young man had asked whether he had evolved sufficiently to contact the White Brotherhood, to which Cayce replied succinctly, "The brother of brothers, the Christ!"[56] In a life reading about a character associated with Jesus, Cayce said that she had been "chosen by those of the Brotherhood—sometimes called the White Brotherhood in the present—as the handmaid or companion of Mary, Jesus and Joseph, in their flight into Egypt."[57] In 1941, Cayce was asked if the Essenes were a branch of the Great White Brotherhood, answering, "In general, yes. Specifically, not altogether."[58] In another 1935 reading, the subject asked if she had ever contacted one of the Masters in a past life, only to be told, "Thou wert of the Great White Brotherhood thine self, in Ohum and Og."[59] The same woman asked in 1941 if she would reestablish contact with the Masters in her present life, and was told, "With the deeper seeking, or the deeper meditations, we find that these may be brought about as *assurances* and are well. As to that which might be *used* as experiences, *not* so well."[60] In 1941, the source told another woman, who asked if Virginia Beach was to be safe (presumably in the war), that it was "the center—and the only seaport and center—of the White Brotherhood."[61]

In late 1943, a man inquired if it would be possible to have conscious communication with the Masters of the Brotherhood, and what could be done to develop this ability. Cayce responded, "If the self is purified of every selfish motive, and if the seeking is that such be given that it may be administered to warn His people. But if it is only for the gratifying of self, no. Possible then, and probable, if the self will sanctify thyself in purpose, in body, in mind." He next inquired as to the likelihood of meeting any of "the brothers" in the flesh, "as Mr. Cayce has done, in this incarnation? If so, where and when?" Cayce replied, "Ye may meet many. For oft doth man entertain angels unawares." Asked how to serve the Brotherhood and fellow man, he replied, "Purifying, dedicating, consecrating self and purpose in the Master—the one Master—Him."[62] The implication of such passages is that questioners' ideas about Masters were exaggerated and distorted, and that the existence of advanced souls should be taken for granted as an ordinary part of life rather than made the object of quasi-religious awe. Cayce shifted the Theosophical emphasis on Masters toward a focus on the immediate accessibility of the Christ Consciousness. While writing *There is a River*, Thomas Sugrue sought readings to clarify the religious teachings in the readings. He offered this definition of Christ Consciousness: "the awareness within each soul, imprinted in pattern on the mind and waiting to be awakened by the will, of the soul's oneness with God," to which Cayce replied "Correct. That's the idea exactly!"[63]

In 1930, a reading for Edwin Blumenthal addressed him as if Jesus were speaking: "Let that mind be in you as was and is *ever* in Me," referring to the Christ Consciousness.[64] He explained that "Jesus the man became aware of the Spirit of the Father through those experiences of the man as he 'went about doing good' . . . [and] received those acknowledgments of the Father that He *was* the one who could, *would*, through those activities, become the Savior of man. First, as 'in whom I am well pleased'; then as 'This is my son, hear ye him!' "[65] The essence of true Christian faith is not in the Jesus consciousness, which "men build as body worship," but rather in the Christ Consciousness, a "universal consciousness of the Father Spirit."[66] There is a seeming disparity in the readings between language describing God in personal terms and passages referring to Creative Forces and other such pantheistic language. This inspired a questioner to ask whether God is an impersonal force or energy, or an intelligent listening mind, which is aware of every individual? The answer, typically Caycean in its attempt to reconcile seeming oppositions, was, "Both! For He is also the energies in the finite moving in material manifestation. He is also the Infinite with the awareness . . . until ye become as a savior, as

eral describing a similarly clad figure who intervened at crucial moments in Cayce's career.

Harmon Bro's 1989 biography, *A Seer Out of Season*, gives an account of a conversation he had with Cayce during research for his doctoral dissertation. Cayce described an inexplicable event that occurred in 1911, after he had discovered that his associates had lied to him and used his abilities for wrong ends. He began to suspect something was amiss when he started to have headaches, which warned him that the readings were not proceeding properly. When he examined the readings transcripts, he could find nothing wrong, so he contacted some of the recipients, only to find that several had received no such reading as appeared in the transcript. Cayce confronted his partners, including his father, and found out that they had sought readings on financial investments and produced fraudulent transcripts to conceal the fact. He ended the partnership with a series of lawsuits that left him with no equipment or money from the studio venture. Thirty years later, Cayce told Bro that he had been warned of the unreliability of his associates by an omen more striking than his headaches:

> [A] tall figure of darker complexion dressed in white and wearing a white turban walked up the stairs to his studio one day, looked him earnestly in the face, and said, "You are with the wrong people." The man then turned and went down the stairs. Cayce was certain he heard his footsteps, but when he recovered his composure enough to run down after him, the townspeople standing on the sidewalk assured him flatly that nobody—absolutely nobody, had come by and entered or left the studio upstairs.[78]

This was the first of several appearances of the mysterious figure at crucial times in Cayce's life; although he initially thought it was a Hindu, the readings later identified him as Persian. During the June 1931 meeting at which the Association for Research and Enlightenment took shape, Edgar saw the same turbaned and robed figure sitting on the landing of the stairs, and was encouraged when the mysterious being nodded during the discussion. No one else saw the man.[79] The final appearance of the figure in white turban and robes occurred in 1932 when Cayce was in New York after being arrested for fortunetelling. He was walking down the street and saw coming toward him the same figure he had seen in Bowling Green more than twenty years earlier:

This time passersby saw the striking sight, and a crowd began to gather. The dark-complected man in white came up to him and then knelt before him, saying nothing. In a few moments scores of people pressed in so tightly to see the strange sight that Cayce had to be rescued from the crush by a nearby policeman. When he looked back, the white-clad figure was gone, and he never saw him again.[80]

These incidents may suggest some reasons for Cayce's assertion that the Great White Brotherhood was in some sense directing him, despite his consistent deflection of questions about the subject. Whatever the mixture of myth and history in these stories, they place Cayce in context as an heir of the modern Theosophical movement inaugurated by Blavatsky. But within that context he was a revisionist, stressing principles from his own Protestant background as correctives to the perceived excesses of the Theosophists. Harmon Bro points out that rather than being awed by his encounters with the man in the turban, Cayce was intrigued and bemused, never knowing what to make of the experiences. Cayce's casual interest in Eastern Masters was never remotely comparable to his lifelong devotion to Jesus Christ, whom he also encountered in dreams and visions.

The Caycean Religious Synthesis

The theology of the readings reconciles New Thought and Theosophy with the ecumenical, noncreedal Protestantism with which Cayce was affiliated in his waking life. Harmon Bro provides valuable evidence concerning the development of Caycean theology in his Ph.D. dissertation (History of religions, University of Chicago) as well as his biography *A Seer Out of Season*. Bro, an ordained minister and graduate student, spent nine months observing Cayce near the end of the seer's life. The most scholarly account of Cayce available, Bro's writings are a milestone in American religious biography. In no other case has such a significant figure been observed firsthand at length and in such detail by an academically trained theologian and historian of religion. Although Bro's perspective has put him at odds with other witnesses who knew Cayce longer than he, as well as with the A.R.E., his works are fundamental to any effort to understand Cayce's theology in historical context. Bro strongly emphasizes the consistency of the readings' theology with mainstream Protestantism, writing that Cayce "presented his ideas as interpretation of the great tradition of his faith, rather than as revelation of a new doctrine or way."[81] Indeed,

Bro initially found Cayce's theology "far too conservative and Christocentric for a Chicago theological student."[82]

In some ways Cayce might seem to be as related to Spiritualism as to New Thought or Theosophy. He was on friendly terms with two of the best-known mediums of his day, Arthur Ford and Eileen Garrett. In his autobiography (co-written by Marguerite Harmon Bro, mother of Cayce's biographer), Ford lauds Cayce as "probably the most gifted man, psychically, I have ever known."[83] Ford, although a Disciples of Christ minister, conformed to traditional Spiritualist mediumship in having a discarnate guide and devoting much of his effort to contacting the spirits of the dead. Cayce, by contrast, was "forever distinguishing himself from mediums and Spiritualism, with which he felt he had far less in common than with the various churches in which he taught Sunday School throughout his life . . . "[84] according to Harmon Bro's dissertation. David Bell points out that "While the readings generally take the truth of Spiritualist phenomena for granted, seekers are usually warned not to become distracted from higher spiritual purposes."[85] Bell adds, however, that Cayce exchanged readings with Eileen Garrett and "cautiously praised her work."[86] Bro commented in his dissertation that a "surprisingly large number" of Cayce's "lifelong associates" were involved in New Thought, Spiritualism, and occultism, "considering Cayce's own lack of background in these areas."[87] But while the readings contain a great many references to Spiritualism, they are usually critical, whereas New Thought and Theosophy are treated with relative respect.

A useful metaphor for the process of synthesis in a new spiritual teaching is offered by Stephen Prothero's biography of Henry Steel Olcott, founding president of the Theosophical Society. In *The White Buddhist*, Prothero argues that Buddhism as understood by Olcott was a " 'creolization' of liberal American Protestantism and traditional Theravada Buddhism."[88] Creole languages combine elements from "host" languages, which dominate the vocabulary, and "substrate" languages, which dominate the grammar and syntax. For example, Haitian patois relies largely on French vocabulary but African structural elements. Similarly, Prothero argues, Olcott's Buddhism used the vocabulary of his Asian host culture but retained the basic assumptions of his native Protestantism. Linguistics theorists note that "individuals seem to be almost as insistent about clinging to inherited grammatical forms as they are comfortable with adopting new vocabularies."[89] Applying this metaphor to Cayce's readings, he can be said to have freely adopted the vocabularies of Theosophy and New Thought while retaining the fundamental logic of American Protestantism.

There appears to be some relationship between the chronological introduction of various new vocabularies in the readings and their overall influence in Cayce's synthesis. For example, osteopathy entered his vocabulary at the beginning of his psychic career, yet one finds thousands of references to it in his readings from 1923–45. When Cayce gave public lectures in Birmingham in 1922, he spoke to the Unity Church as well as the Theosophical Society; this was his first time speaking outside his own church circles.[90] In the closing years of his life, New Thought and Theosophy were still the most recognizable elements in his theology apart from his native Protestantism. An example of this creolization would be the way in which Cayce takes the acquired vocabulary of karma and interprets it in terms of the Law vs. Grace theme in Disciples theology.[91]

In a letter to an inquirer, Cayce wrote, "Unity is doing a very wonderful work, I think. For many years I have been in touch with some of their leaders and teachers. We gave some information once for Mr. Fillmore."[92] Bell notes that Cayce views Divine Science as favorably as Unity, only Christian Science among the mental healing groups being criticized in the readings.[93] A cooperative relationship between Unity and the A.R.E. has continued to the present, with jointly sponsored programs occasionally offered. Part of the natural affinity between the two may be due to Unity's receptivity to holistic medicine, in juxtaposition to Christian Science's general rejection of material healing. But it is also noteworthy that the Fillmores had studied Theosophy as well as Christian Science, and their own synthesis can be seen as a creolization of the two.

Harmon Bro emphasizes Cayce's differences from the occultist milieu, citing his "open, non-esoteric symplicity of manner in counseling . . . his strongly Christocentric theology, together with his consistent attempts to avoid becoming the center of a religious cult or 'ism.' "[94] Although slightly prepared by his associations with occultists during his 1922 lecture tour, Cayce was "severely shocked by the apparent unorthodoxy" of the doctrines that came through the readings in response to Lammers's questions in 1923, according to family members interviewed by Bro.[95] But by the time Bro met Cayce, his attitude toward the Disciples of Christ was one of "pleasant and thoughtful reminiscence rather than of resurrected partisanship."[96] Although years of attendance at a Presbyterian church must have played some role in this change, one must also weigh the effect of years of immersion in the atmosphere of New Thought, Theosophy, and Spiritualism which pervaded the A.R.E. membership.

There appears to have been greater contact between the A.R.E. and some Christian-oriented offshoots of the Theosophical Society than with the T.S. itself. Particularly noteworthy in this regard is a cordial relationship with Anthroposophy. Since 1973, the A.R.E. has invited Anthroposophic leaders to speak at conferences; in 1996, one conference was dominated by Anthroposophical speakers. Mark Thurston, an Executive Director of the A.R.E., is also a member of the Anthroposophical Society. As early as 1932, Anthroposophists Helene and Ernest Zentgraff of Staten Island were hosts to the Cayces and Gladys Davis during a trip to New York.[97] The Anthroposophical Society founder Rudolf Steiner had formerly been head of the German Section of the Theosophical Society, and his system retains much of the vocabulary of Blavatskian Theosophy. But Steiner, like Cayce, sees the Christ as the central figure in human history, in sharp distinction to the Buddhist Blavatsky.[98] The Cayce CD-ROM includes many references to Steiner, but almost all are in correspondence rather than the readings. One passage endorses Steiner's clairvoyance "in a trend, not as in toto, but a VISION of an entity as reading records of that as happened in space and time."[99] Another refers to the Anthroposophical Society, commenting on "phases of same that are excellent" yet advising that particular counselee to approach it "but not as an identified member."[100] Steiner was mentioned in an A.R.E. Congress by Thomas Sugrue, and A.R.E. member Ralph Courtney questioned the readings about Steiner's reform plans.[101] Steiner's books *Atlantis & Lemuria* and *Theosophy* are approvingly cited in the readings.[102] Some Anthroposophists thought they saw references to Cayce in Steiner's writings; similar suggestions were made by Alice Bailey disciples. Although there are eleven references to Bailey in eight documents on the CD-ROM, none is in the readings themselves. Bailey, like Steiner, accepts most of Blavatskian Theosophy but places Jesus Christ at the center of the occult hierarchy. There is some overlap between the ranks of Bailey disciples and A.R.E. members at present, understandably in light of their common thread of "creolization." Bailey, like Steiner and Cayce, adopted the Blavatskian vocabulary while retaining the basic assumptions of Christianity; unlike them she continued Blavatsky's strong emphasis on the Masters as objects of devotion.

Among the more intimately revealing readings are those in which Cayce submitted his own dreams for interpretation. In 1931, after the collapse of his hospital and university and the founding of the A.R.E., Cayce dreamed of "trying to fix the yard" and finding it "all undermined with refuse and seeping water."[103] The reading interpreted this as a sign of undermining conditions in his life, but then gave the assurance that "each and every attempt in any direction is grounded, and *founded,* in the Christ Jesus, for *He* is the foundation, the author, the finisher, of all good that may come to anyone through these channels."[104] No matter how far afield his occult explorations took him, Cayce remained firmly committed to the faith of his childhood. In a dream from late 1942, Cayce saw himself in heaven with Jesus and the evangelists Dwight Moody (whom Cayce had met as a teenager) and Sam Jones. From a cloud and lightning came a voice saying "Who will warn my children?" Jesus offered to do so, but the voice of God said it was not yet time. After Moody suggested Cayce to be the message bearer, Jesus said "Father, Cayce will warn my brethren."[105] But if Cayce saw himself as a warner, the content of the readings suggests that his primary warning was of the need for direct mystical experience as a means of revivifying a Christianity that had become detached from its paracletic roots.

Some light may be shed on the way Cayce synthesized various religious elements by examining his theology from the standpoint of the sociology of knowledge. This subdiscipline originated in Germany in the 1920s and, in the words of Peter Berger, "is concerned with studying the relationship between human thought and the social conditions under which it occurs."[106] Berger has applied the sociology of knowledge to American Protestantism in several books, two of which are particularly relevant to the Cayce phenomenon. In *A Rumor of Angels* he explores the "plausibility structures" of twentieth-century America, competing networks of assumptions about what ideas are credible. The sociology of knowledge postulates that "the plausibility, in the sense of what people actually find credible, of views of reality depends upon the social support they receive."[107]

Edgar Cayce was almost inevitably drawn into the company of Theosophists, New Thought disciples, Anthroposophists, and Spiritualists by the nature of his gift. Although he retained a lifelong attachment to the church, the social support he needed could not be found in its ranks. Struggling to understand himself and his confusing psychic experiences, he needed the support of people whose "plausibility structures" included clairvoyance, telepathy, and spiritual healing. First in Birmingham and later in Dayton, he found himself in a congenial atmosphere that encouraged him to develop his ability in new ways. But once Cayce began to immerse himself in the milieu of esoteric spirituality, he was at great pains to reconcile the plausibility structures of his Protestant upbringing with the shocking new ideas of reincarnation, astrology, Atlantis, and so on. Cayce's Christianity after 1923 was in continual dialogue with alternate plausibility structures. His boyhood faith was challenged by its lack of adequate explanation of his own experience. But as he reached out to New Thought, Theosophy, and other unorthodox movements for explanations, he found many ideas and emphases that he considered unacceptable. The theology of the readings after 1923 was constructed through dialogue between the entranced Cayce and a succession of thousands of counselees. The mixture of Protestants, Catholics, Jews, Quakers, Spiritualists, Theosophists, Christian Scientists, and others who sought readings helped to determine the shape of the Christology that developed over the years. (Mainstream Christians always were the majority of counselees; "Protestant" appears 1,305 times on the CD-ROM and "Catholic" 300 times.) This need not imply a reductionist judgment that there was "nothing more than" this dialogue at work. There is a continuing tension in the sociology of knowledge between reductionist and anti-reductionist approaches, between those who hold that texts have meanings that are irreducible to their contexts and the interests of their authors and those who hold that motives and context are all-important. Although Cayce may have had experienced mystical enlightenment and transcendence, he still had to convey its message to people situated in a particular social setting. During his lifetime and throughout the twentieth century, religion was under assault from the competing claims of secular culture. Moreover, twentieth-century American Christianity has also been faced with alternative plausibility structures in the form of Eastern religions, first mediated largely through Theosophy and related movements but more recently competing directly in the marketplace of ideas.

The twentieth-century search for a new understanding of Christianity is addressed by Berger's *The Heretical Imperative*, which further develops themes introduced in *A Rumor of Angels*. Describing the modern situation as one in which religious identity is a matter of choice rather than inheritance, Berger explores three alternative paths of religious affirmation. In a pluralistic world with many possible choices, no religion can survive simply by asserting itself as the only alternative. The word "heresy" is derived from the Greek *harein* (to choose), so Berger calls the present need for religious adaptation the heretical imperative. The reductive possibility is the redefinition of religion in terms of the secular worldview; Berger calls this "cognitive bargaining" and finds an example in the "demythologizing" theology of Rudolf Bultmann. Mainstream Protestantism since the nineteenth century has been faced with the progressive encroachment of science into realms previously claimed by religion. The tendency of its liberal wing has been to negotiate terms under which religion can survive in a scientific world. A second alternative is the deductive possibility, which simply reaffirms tradition despite the challenges of modernity. The neo-orthodox theology of Karl Barth is a Protestant example of this strategy, which makes leaps of faith across the chasms of scientific doubt. In cruder form, fundamentalism in any religion exemplifies this strategy. The third, implicitly favored, alternative is the inductive possibility. Berger sees Friedrich Schleiermacher as the chief Protestant exemplar of this strategy, which emphasizes a return to the experiential roots of a tradition in order to revivify it. Rather than yielding ground to secularism or blindly affirming orthodoxy, the inductive possibility redefines religion in the face of modernity through the retracing of history and the return to direct experience.[108]

In the context of Berger's model, the Christianity of Cayce adheres to the inductive option. While using the grammar of orthodoxy, Cayce anchors its meaning in direct mystical experience, and claims to recapture the original teachings of Jesus. The specific historical claims made about Jesus in the readings are addressed in chapter 3. The more general claim that Cayce's teachings are a return to a lost understanding of true Christianity relates him to the revival of interest in Gnosticism.

An American Gnostic

Asked if Gnosticism was the closest form of Christianity to that coming through the readings, Cayce answered, "this is a parallel, and was the commonly accepted one until there began to be set rules in which there were the attempts to take shortcuts. And there are none in Christianity!"[109] It is not clear what is meant by "shortcuts," but Harmon Bro's criticisms of the A.R.E. suggest some possibilities. As early as 1955, Bro was condemning "changes that have occurred in the direction of gnostic occultism" after Cayce's death, saying that Cayce himself held these tendencies in check.[110] Indeed, Bro blames "the gnostic expressions of his associates" for repelling people from the movement.[111] His negative attitude toward Gnosticism seems to be based on the social disengagement of some early Christian Gnostics, who sought to extricate themselves from an evil world with no thought of the fate of humanity as a whole. Bro, with a background in the American Protestant tradition of social engagement, has criticized the A.R.E. as a haven for occultists who have emphasized the "information" in the Cayce readings at the expense of implementation of their ideals. The "shortcuts" to which the above-quoted reading refers are, according to this outlook, practices that seek individual salvation rather than redemption of all humanity. But there are so many parallels between Caycean Christology and Gnosticism that it seems ill-advised to use "gnostic" as a term of sweeping condemnation.

An incisive analysis of the role of Gnostic themes in American religious consciousness is found in Harold Bloom's 1992 study *The American Religion*. Although Bloom does not address the Cayce phenomenon directly, much of his insightful criticism seems more applicable to Cayce than to the religious figures explicitly examined. For example, in his discussions of Mormonism, Christian Science, and Seventh-day Adventism, Bloom emphasizes the American penchant for expanding the scriptures either outright or implicitly. Yet no body of work produced by any American-born religious founder exceeds the Cayce readings in volume, complexity, or Biblical style. Bloom concludes that "The essence of the American is the belief that God loves her or him, a conviction shared by nearly nine out of ten of us, according to a Gallup poll."[112] Nowhere can there be found a more consistent, unqualified, and personally specific testimony to the message that "God loves you" than in the Cayce readings. By addressing each individual in his or her uniqueness, responding to specific needs of body, mind, and soul, and reassuring all of their eternal oneness with the Father, Cayce epitomizes this strain of the American religious consciousness.

Bloom discerns in American religion an obsession with the question "What makes us free?" in addition to the universal questions "Where were we?" and "where are we journeying?"[113] Cayce's answers to these questions are a restatement of themes found in Gnosticism, for example "That in the material world is a shadow of that in the celestial or spiritual world."[114] Our origin is as sparks of divinity prior to the creation of the universe. We have become involved in material existence through a series of stages of increasing forgetfulness, and we are now on a return pilgrimage back to the source:

> Each soul is a portion of the Divine. Motivating that soul-body is the spirit of divinity. The soul is a companion of, a motivative influence in, the activities of an entity throughout its experiences in whatever sphere of consciousness it may attain perception. Hence each soul is a universe in itself.[115]

What makes us free is the Christ Consciousness, which illumines the path back to the Creator:

> And it is for that purpose that He came into the earth; that we, as soul-entities, might know ourselves to be ourselves, and yet one with Him; as He, the Master, the Christ, knew Himself to be Himself and yet one with the Father.[116]

Combining the definitions given at the beginning of this chapter, Cayce's teachings are theosophical in that they attempt to reconstitute primordial Christianity through evoking an ahistorical, paracletic return of the soul to its source (Versluis), and thereby reconciling the earthly and divine realms (Faivre). This is distinct from some forms of Gnosticism in that theosophy by definition appreciates and honors the world as a divine expression, rather than seeing it as the fallen creation of an inferior or malevolent god. In the words of the readings:

> [A]ll souls stand as ONE before that Universal Consciousness, that Throne of grace, of mercy, that has brought the souls of men into materiality in body, that there might be an awareness more and more of *their* relationship—yea, their kinship to that *source* of right, justice, mercy, patience, long-suffering, love.[117]

Bloom finds two consistent factors in every authentically American religion: finding God within the self, in "absolute isolation as a spark of God floating in a sea of space," and salvation attained through a "one-on-one act of confrontation."[118] The essential drive in American religion is thus "to know, rather than to believe or to trust."[119] Tracing these themes through the largest and most influential American-born sects, Bloom finds a Gnostic thread linking them all, an emphasis on the self as originating in a primordial union with divinity prior to the creation of the world. While this seems descriptive of the Cayce readings, it does not emphasize as he did the crucial element of sacrificial love and service. Although "each entity, each soul, is in the process of evolution toward the First Cause,"[120] " . . . *each* and every soul *must become, must be,* the *savior* of some soul! to even *comprehend* the purpose of the entrance of the Son *into* the earth—that man might have the closer walk with, yea the open door to, the very heart of the living God!"[121]

The Cosmic Christ, described by Burton Mack as a "power that pulsates throughout the world making all of time and space eternally present around us,"[122] is the hero of the Gospel of John, which Cayce emphasized more than any other book of the Bible. According to Richard Drummond, the readings "tend to follow the Johannine tradition more than the synoptic, both biographically and theologically."[123] Drummond is the author of *Unto the Churches* and *A Life of Jesus the Christ,* the two most scholarly studies of Cayce's Christianity yet published. An ordained Presbyterian minister, Drummond served as a missionary and has taught religious studies and classics at universities in Japan and the United States. A longtime student of the readings,

Drummond regards them as useful to scholars of Christian origins, commenting that "Clairvoyance is here treated as one potentially legitimate element in a process of interdisciplinary studies, whereby the participants continue to make use of traditional academic disciplines . . . "[124] Drummond presents Cayce's readings about Jesus in the context of Biblical scholarship and evangelical belief. While acknowledging the unconventional nature of some of Cayce's teachings, Drummond maintains that the readings "are equal to any Protestant conservative evangelical in their strong emphasis upon the theological priority of God's love and grace in action, supremely manifested in Jesus the Christ."[125] Although he stresses the readings' general compatibility with Christian orthodoxy, Drummond presents the Gnostics in a much more favorable light than is typically encountered in mainstream church sources. Rudolf Steiner and Carl Jung praised the Gnostics as highly as did Cayce, which led Drummond to reconsider their significance. Pointing out that few people called themselves Gnostics, and that many diverse groups were later labeled such by those who sought to condemn them as heretics, he argues that the entire range of Gnostic thought has been unfairly condemned. This is due in part to the paucity of primary sources and the extreme anti-Gnostic bias found in many accounts. Only with the discovery of the Nag Hammadi library has it become possible to understand the Gnostics in their own terms. Few of them practiced the extremes of asceticism and licentiousness that were typical of a handful of groups. Contrary to popular belief, only a minority of Christian Gnostics believed the world to have been created by a rebellious being or beings opposed to the will of the highest God. The majority "averred the material creation through mediation but believed the mediators to have acted in accord with the will of the Highest."[126] The most important distinction of the Gnostics was their perception of salvation as "a repeatable 'now,' as a meaningful process of spiritual and moral growth both on earth and in the unseen realms beyond . . . envisaged as possibly extending through a number of lives on earth and ultimately through the heavenly spheres."[127] Cayce's views of creation and salvation accord with those of the Gnostics, which might help explain his positive references to them.

In addition to thousands of readings expounding Christian doctrines in neo-Theosophical, neo-Gnostic language, Cayce also gave a detailed description of the historical Jesus. Chapter 3 examines Cayce's descriptions of the past and future, with emphasis on the times and places receiving the greatest attention in the readings.

3.1

Edgar Cayce, 1932.

Photograph courtesy of the Edgar Cayce Foundation. Copyrighted 1978
Edgar Cayce Foundation. All rights reserved. Used by permission.

3

Clairvoyant Time Traveler

"Prophet" is the word most associated with Edgar Cayce by the reading public since the 1967 publication of Jess Stearn's *The Sleeping Prophet*. Cayce's predictions of the future are fodder for both his admirers and his critics, since many of them remain unfulfilled although several have been successful. The clairvoyant time travel in the readings, however, is devoted overwhelmingly to the past. In his life readings, Cayce gives a panoramic view of history from Atlantis through modern times. The inscrutable mystery of the Cayce readings is nowhere more challenging than in those devoted to the past and the future. Some of the strongest evidence for Cayce's paranormal ability is found in his predictions, but some of the greatest obstacles to belief in his reliability are found in his descriptions of the past and future. The readings give pause to anyone in search of simple answers about the potentials of human consciousness, from uncritical admirers to absolute skeptics.

The origin of humanity, according to the readings, was in the spiritual realm. Echoing Gnostic and theosophical themes, Cayce teaches that souls "fell" into earthly existence by projecting themselves into material vehicles and becoming entangled in matter. This eventually caused humanity to forget its origin in the spiritual realm and its ultimate return to its divine source.[1] From the beginning of human existence on Earth until our eventual reunion with God, history evolves through a series of cyclical phases.[2]

The readings' cosmology is emanationist, teaching that light is "that from which, through which, in which may be found all things, out of which all things come."[3] This echoes a broad consensus in Western mystical traditions, from Neoplatonism through Suhrawardi. There is relatively little detail in the readings, however, about the evolution of the cosmos and the earth prior to the arrival of humanity. Cayce teaches that humanity appeared after animals, which included the monsters of legend; satyrs, mermaids, and unicorns were all historical, according to the readings.[4] Humanity entered the earth as a group, with five races simultaneously appearing in Atlantis, "Gobi, India, in Carpathia, or in that known as the Andes, and that known as in the Western plains of what is now called America."[5] Cayce states emphatically that "Man appeared not from that already created . . . Man DID NOT descend from the monkey . . . "[6] Like Blavatsky, he accepts the evolution of the physical human form while insisting that the human spirit and soul arrived from a spiritual realm to inhabit the physical form at a particular point in history. The spiritual beings who incarnated in fleshly bodies were immortal until death "became man's portion" after "sin entered—that is, away from the face of the Maker . . . "[7] The general pattern of a spiritual humanity descending into earthly bodies and becoming mortal is found in Blavatskian Theosophy and many of its offshoots; the roots of such an "involutionary" doctrine may be found in Gnosticism and its antecedents.[8]

The Lost Continent

There is far more detail in the readings concerning the history of Atlantis than any of the other alleged simultaneous sites of earliest humanity. The credibility of the existence of Atlantis is described in a curiously equivocal way in reading 364–1:

> Atlantis as a continent is a legendary tale. Whether or not that which has been received through psychic sources has for its basis those few lines given by Plato, or the references made in the Holy Writ that the earth was divided, depends upon the trends of individual minds. . . . There has been considerable given respecting such a lost continent by those channels such as the writer of Two Planets, or Atlantis—or Poseidia and Lemuria—that has been published through some Theosophical literature. As to whether this information is true or not, depends upon the credence individuals give to this class of information.[9]

Coming from the source of the most elaborate and detailed depiction of Atlantis that has ever appeared, this passage is so diffident as to raise immediate questions. How can the truth or falsehood of the lost continent be dependent on the attitudes of twentieth-century readers? Why was Cayce, despite his voluminous descriptions of Atlantis, so indefinite about their veracity? If the Atlantean material is of such questionable reliability according to Cayce himself, what implications does this have for the rest of the historical material channeled through the same source? Before exploring these questions, it may be helpful to survey the readings' description of Atlantis.

In his first book on the subject, Edgar Evans Cayce points out the "amazing" internal consistency of the readings about Atlantis.[10] Equally striking is the readings' consistency with previously published sources describing Atlantis, notably Blavatsky's *The Secret Doctrine*. Like Blavatsky, the Cayce readings teach that Atlantis was as large as Europe, inhabited by giants, had a highly advanced science and technology, extended from the area of the Caribbean to the opposite shores of the present Atlantic Ocean, existed many millions of years ago, and was not finally destroyed until around 10,000 B.C.[11] Some of the details Cayce gave about Atlantis, however, appear to have originated with him. The lifespan of Atlanteans was 1,000 years.[12] Atlanteans dressed in white and purple linen[13] and ate "corn meal and figs and dates prepared together with goat's milk."[14] Other elements of Cayce's Atlantis are found in Oliver's *Dweller on Two Planets*. "Transmission of thought through ether" was taught as a formal study.[15] As a result, some Atlanteans misused psychic powers in controlling one another.[16] A recurring theme in the readings is the struggle between two factions with very different approaches to the use of psychic powers. The children of the Law of One used "concentration of thought for the use of the universal forces, through the guidance or direction of the saints" and could thereby "impart understanding and knowledge to the group thus gathered."[17] But while the followers of the Law of One observed altruistic standards of right and wrong, their opponents, the "Sons of Belial," had "no standard, save of self, self-aggrandizement."[18] The Law of One is equated with the Christ Consciousness, which is said to have incarnated in Atlantis as Amilius.[19] These are all similar to emphases in Oliver's work.

Atlanteans' superiority to contemporary humanity extended beyond their physical size, lifespan, and spiritual qualities. According to Cayce, Atlantis was extremely advanced in a technological sense as well. Atlantean technology included engineering of buildings and public works, using advanced metallurgy involving the lost art of tempering aluminum and uranium with iron.[20] Their medical technology included a machine that could "change the blood" and an "electrical knife" which would be used for "bloodless surgery."[21] Elephant hides were used to make balloons powered by gases, which were able to travel underwater as well as in the air.[22] A power source called "the Crystal" was contained in a dome, where it collected solar energy and from which power was distributed. In addition to solar power, the crystal used "heat from within the elements of the earth itself."[23] The first of three destructions of Atlantis was caused by power plants "tuned too high" which "broke up the land into the isles."[24] A crystal was used in directing airplanes that could also become submarines.[25]

One of the curious aspects of Cayce's description of Atlantis is the way it seems to foreshadow technological developments of our own century, occurring mainly after Cayce's death. One reading explicitly comments on the parallels between Atlantis and our own technical achievements:

> [T]here was the application of much of that being discovered or rather rediscovered today, in the application of power to modes of transit as well as the use of nature's means for a helpful force in giving greater crops for individual consumption. Also they were periods when a great deal of thought was given as to conveniences of every nature.[26]

Atlanteans had developed photography, and through some means could read "inscriptions through walls—even at distances"; they could also overcome "the forces of nature or gravity itself" through the "mighty, the terrible crystal."[27] Cayce predicted that humanity would rediscover, within twenty-five years, the "Death Ray, or the supercosmic ray."[28] This may be related to "the ray that makes for disintegration of the atom," which is attributed to the Atlanteans in the readings.[29] Atlanteans had built equipment that could "transpose or build up the elements about them" as well as "transpose them bodily from one portion of the universe to the other, *through* the uses of not only those *recently* rediscovered gases, and those of the electrical and aeriatic formations in the breaking up of the atomic forces to produce impelling force [for] travel . . . lifting large weights, or of changing the faces or forces of nature itself . . . "[30]

According to the readings, Atlantis coexisted with other civilizations. Lemuria, a continent in the Pacific, was alleged to have disappeared before Atlantis, in a series of cataclysms lasting 200,000 years.[31] After the second major cataclysm in Atlantis around 28,000 B.C., there was a series of migrations to other areas. The readings claim that Central American ruins derived from Atlantean migrations, as did Inca civilization. They assert that the Mound Builders of the Ohio and Mississippi valleys were "the second generation of Atlanteans who struggled northward from Yucatan."[32] After these migrations, there was continued contact among the various migrant populations, according to Cayce. Civilizations in what is now the southwestern United States were associated with those "in Egypt, the Gobi, the Og—cooperated in one great cause."[33] In addition to Central America and the United States, evidence of Atlantean migration is allegedly present in the Pyrenees and Morocco.[34] No other country, however, was as in-

debted to the Atlanteans as ancient Egypt. These claims are reminiscent of Ignatius Donnelly's *Atlantis,* which bases its arguments on
alleged similarities between cultures and place names of Central and
South American Indian cultures and those of Egypt.[35]

The Search for Ra Ta

The most detailed depiction of any past culture in the Cayce
readings is that of Egypt around 10,500 B.C. The central character in
these readings is Ra Ta, a young priest from the Caucasus region who
advised his king Arart that his tribe would successfully invade Egypt
and make it the most powerful nation on earth.[36] The invaders are
described as light skinned, whereas the indigenous Egyptians were
dark. Strife between the two groups was reduced by the abdication of
King Arart in favor of his son Araaraat. Ra Ta was a past life of Edgar
Cayce, and Araaraat his son Hugh Lynn. Atlantean immigrants came
to Egypt during Araaraat's long reign; Egypt was as culturally advanced as Atlantis had been, with similar accomplishments in science,
engineering, and the arts.[37] Ra Ta became the High Priest of Egypt and
in that role promoted the Law of One. "Ra Ta was not a lord, not a god,
but a teacher, an instructor, an interpreter."[38] He was obsessed with
what we now call genetic engineering, hoping thereby to produce perfect human bodies. Ra Ta's goal was "a purer, a better race."[39] Trade was
carried on during this period with the Atlantean remnant island called
Poseidia, and with Europe, Asia, and the Americas.[40] Ra Ta's great con-
tribution in this period was the construction of the Temple of Sacrifice
and the Temple Beautiful. The former is described as "that wherein the
body was shed of the animal representations through the sacrificing of
the desires of the appetite, through the *changing* of self in the temple
service"; the latter as the place where "appurtenances that would hinder,"
such as feathers and claws, disappeared.[41] Egypt, like Atlantis, had
produced hybrid human/animal monsters with a variety of deformi-
ties. The appendages were symbolic of "the faults, the virtues of man,
in all his seven stages of development."[42] The Temple of Sacrifice is
described by an A.R.E. author as a hospital in which treatments included "surgery, medicines, electrical therapy, massage, spinal adjustments and the like."[43] Temple Beautiful priests and priestesses provided
instruction in music, agriculture, fabric crafts, and pottery.[44] The
Alexandrian library was founded during the Ra Ta period.[45]

Gertrude Cayce was identified as Isris, a temple dancer who
became involved in a plot to seduce Ra Ta which resulted in his ban-
ishment by the young king. She was exiled with him to Abyssinia, but

after nine years a series of uprisings led Araaraat to invite them back to Egypt. After their return, Ra Ta became simply Ra, and Isris became Isis.[46] The most important accomplishments of Ra's career occurred after his return, when he planned construction of Great Pyramid and several subsidiary buildings. The Sphinx, begun as a monument to Araaraat, was under Ra's direction transformed into a spiritual symbol of the relationship between animal and spiritual elements in human development.[47] The Great Pyramid was planned by Ra, but built by Hermes, "a descendant of Hermes Trismegistus, who had returned with the Priest from the Nubian land of exile."[48] Its role was as a ceremonial center for initiation into the mysteries. Construction was by means of levitation of stones through application of occult laws. In its construction is encoded a forecast of the evolution of humanity from the time of Ra through 1998. The records preserved in a special hall of records between the Sphinx and the Great Pyramid will be found when mankind is ready for their discovery. These are both records brought from Atlantis and those of the original Egyptian civilization. The astronomy and astrology of ancient Egypt are allegedly encoded in the monuments planned by Ra. The readings assert that "Accurate imaginary lines can be drawn from the opening of the Great Pyramid to the second star in the Big Dipper, called Polaris ... the system through which the soul takes its flight ... "[49] In a similar reference, Cayce stated that "When the lines about the earth are considered from the mathematical precisions, it will be found that the center is nigh unto where the Great Pyramid, which was begun then, is still located."[50]

In 1985, cover stories in three consecutive issues of *Venture Inward* dealt with evidence that tends to undermine the reliability of the readings on Egypt. The first two issues contained a two-part interview with Mark Lehner, a young Egyptologist whose research was inspired by the Cayce readings. The January/February cover story gives a general description of Lehner's decade of research on the Sphinx and the Pyramids, which made him "probably the leading American authority" on the subject.[51] Asked by interviewer A. Robert Smith about the roots of his fascination with Egypt, Lehner explained that the Edgar Cayce readings provided the initial impetus to specialize in Egyptology. Lehner's first book, *The Egyptian Heritage,* was published by A.R.E. Press in 1974, and describes the readings' internally consistent, coherent description of a civilization in Egypt in 10,500 B.C. that coexisted with the end of Atlantean civilization.[52] Comparing the readings with scientific consensus about Egyptian history as well as with legendary material, Lehner found far more correspondence with the latter. Arab legends about Hermes building the Great Pyramid as a repository of knowledge and Jewish legends about "an evil race of watchers that existed before the flood and ... were destroyed" are both echoed in the Cayce readings.[53] But the scholarly consensus of the date of the monuments is about 8,000 years more recent than that given in the readings. Lehner concludes that a civilization of the complexity and sophistication depicted in the readings would have left some residue, and there is no such evidence that would support Cayce's descriptions. The Hall of Records which Cayce alleged to be reachable through a passage leading from the right paw of the Sphinx is said to contain evidence of Atlantis. Other artifacts from 10,500 B.C. are alleged to be around the site. But the only passage Lehner found was in the rear of the Sphinx, and reached a dead end at fifteen feet.[54] The Edgar Cayce Foundation funded a "remote sensing survey of the Sphinx and the large temple in front of the Sphinx" in 1977, but no passage was discovered.[55] Lehner concludes the first interview by saying that "We have oodles of information out there from archaeological remains, and it all adds up to the culture of the 4th dynasty. The archaeological question is, if there was a culture and a civilization of such magnitude, even it was 8,000 years earlier, where is its pottery, where is its garbage, where are the bodies, inscriptions and so on? It cannot have disappeared without a trace."[56] In the followup interview, Lehner comments that there is tremendous public interest in channeled material about ancient Egypt, which makes Cayce's material interesting as a cultural phenomenon despite its scholarly implausibility. He comments that while "struggling to find the *meaning* of the Cayce information on Egypt if it is not literal truth," he had considered that the truths might be "literary" rather than literal: "Maybe he was reading more the mythical traditions and legends and projecting people's past lives into that plane of legendary history instead of reading what literally happened. Maybe it should be understood more on the level of archetypes."[57] Lehner also acknowledged the possibility that the readings would be vindicated by further research, and that Cayce's past-life readings might be correct except for their dates. But he found it troubling that none of the recorded names from ancient Egypt appears in the readings, and that none of the names in the readings is recognizably Egyptian.[58] This raised the question of just what Cayce's Akashic records were, and how reliable. Lehner comments that "all the data that I thought corroborated or paralleled the Cayce readings" was from myths and legends, while all the negative evidence was "archaeological data—hardcore physical, three-dimensional stuff."[59] He did nonetheless find general similarities between the fourth dynasty and the Cayce readings, particularly concerning the worship of Ra, the sun god.[60] Moreover, there is a dispute between the king and the priests of Ra in legendary accounts of Khufu, as well as in the Cayce readings.[61] Lehner mentions a project at A.R.E. to investigate more recent lives in the readings, examining records to see if names and dates given could be confirmed. He comments, "suppose he has some good hits in those periods, one possible explanation for the Egyptian matter is that the further back in time he went the harder it was to . . . read literal history."[62] In response to a question about his own experience as an A.R.E. member, Lehner said, "I'm not as secure even in my belief structures and not sure that I know as much as I thought I once knew."[63] In his closing remarks, Lehner comments that "The Ra Ta Egypt story in some sense is the myth of this organization," and that perhaps "one's perception of that myth changes, and can grow and mature during the growth of an organization."[64] The third consecutive issue with a cover story about Egyptian history notes that a radiocarbon dating study of the Great Pyramid funded by the Edgar Cayce Foundation confirmed neither Cayce's date for its construction nor the generally accepted date of 2,500 B.C., but rather resulted in an average date of 2,900 B.C., still far closer to conventional estimates than to the Cayce readings.[65] Responding to criticisms in a subsequent issue, Lehner remarked that "none of the names nor the remains of the kings in the Cayce story of Egypt have ever been found at Giza or anywhere else in Egypt . . . archaeologically it is impossible that such a society could disappear without a trace save for its Earth-commensurate measurements in the Great Pyramid."[66]

Although ultimately disappointing, the Egypt project funded by A.R.E. provides strong evidence of the organization's willingness to examine the readings objectively. Lehner had been mentored as a young man by Hugh Lynn and Charles Thomas Cayce, and an A.R.E. couple, Arch and Ann Ogden of Florida, had funded his education in Cairo at the urging of the elder Cayce.[67] Later, Hugh Lynn was instrumental in furthering the graduate education of Zahi Hawass, now the Egyptian government official in charge of the Giza site, in Egyptology at the University of Pennsylvania.[68] Hugh Lynn Cayce devoted considerable time and effort to the attempt to "verify the Ra Ta myth with a stunning archaeological discovery," according to his biographer A. Robert Smith.[69] This was motivated in part by his own alleged past life as the young King Araaraat. During the 1970s, the A.R.E. also supported research at the Nag Hammadi site, and sent Lehner to participate in a Claremont Graduate School dig.[70] Edgar Evans Cayce, an engineer, was as keenly interested in the archaeological research as were his brother and nephew.

Those who retain hope that Cayce will be at least partly confirmed in his readings on Egypt and Atlantis can find comfort in several recent popular works. Robert Bauval's *The Orion Mystery* uses astronomy in an attempt to prove that the Giza pyramids were planned around 10,500 B.C., although not built until millennia later.[71] Pursuing a suggestion found in the works of R. Schwaller de Lubicz that the Sphinx showed signs of water erosion, amateur Egyptologist John Anthony West obtained confirmation of this possibility from geologist Robert Schoch. Although receiving support from some geologists, Schoch's hypothesis, which implies the Sphinx to be at least 7,000 years old, has been universally rejected by professional Egyptologists.[72] Interestingly, an article by Richard Heinberg on these developments now identifies Lehner as a leader of "the establishment opposition to West, Schoch, and Bauval" and as a "former Cayce-ite."[73] In an interview for *Venture Inward,* Schoch estimated the age of the Sphinx at 7–9,000 years, noting that John Anthony West believes its age to be 12–17,000 years. Schoch comments that "you can explain the weathering, in terms of 5,000 to 7,000 B.C."[74] Whatever modifications may eventually be made in the scholarly consensus about ancient Egypt, it is almost certain that most of the Cayce material on the subject will remain unverified.

The Life of Christ

In addition to his theological and theosophical interpretations of Jesus, Cayce's readings give details on early Christian history. Many people who sought life readings were told that they had been witnesses to the life of Jesus, and a consistent picture emerges from the many readings in which such accounts are found. Cayce portrays an Essene community that prepared for the advent of Jesus, and describes Mary and Joseph as members of this group. Although many of his details of the public ministry of Jesus parallel the Bible, Cayce portrays the savior's early life in a decidedly unorthodox manner. Jesus allegedly traveled to Egypt and India for initiation into esoteric traditions there, and broadened his perspective beyond his Essene origins. As a spiritual teacher, "John was more the Essene than Jesus. Jesus held rather to the spirit of the law and John to the letter of same . . . "[75]

The hypothesis of Essene influence on Jesus was not taken seriously by many scholars of Cayce's time, but has gained credibility with the discovery of the Dead Sea scrolls. James Charlesworth comments, in the introduction to a collection of articles entitled *Jesus and the Dead Sea Scrolls,* that the scrolls clarify "not only Jesus' time but also his life and teachings."[76] Elsewhere he writes that "The Qumran covenanters are almost certainly one of the Essene groups, probably the strictest."[77] After elaborating twenty-four major similarities between Jesus and the Qumran group and twenty-seven important differences, Charlesworth concludes that Jesus was neither an Essene nor "significantly influenced" by them, but was probably influenced by them in minor ways:

> He could have shared their fondness for the same scriptural books, and been influenced by their pneumatic, eschatological, and messianic exegesis. He may have inherited from Essenes the idea of redemption eschatologically for "the Poor," sharing of possessions, and condemnation of divorce; the technical terms "sons of light"; and the concept of "the Holy Spirit" . . . [but] Jesus would have rejected the Essenes' calendar, strict conservatism, concept of purity, and rigid binding rules. He would have abhorred— and may well have castigated—their rules for hating, their swearing and their dehumanizing understanding of the Sabbath.[78]

This judgment coheres well with Cayce's portrayal of Jesus, but there do not appear to be any surprising "hits" that would indicate his access to specific confirmable details of the period. The Essenes and their relationship to the Qumran sect remain mysterious despite advances in scholarship. There is definite evidence of similarities between the Qumran covenanters and John the Baptist. But proximity, similarly apocalyptic themes and the practice of baptism do not necessarily indicate direct influence.[79] And since the relationship of the Qumran group to the mainstream Essenes is also unclear, Cayce's claims about Essene influence on Jesus and John remain unconfirmed.

David Bell's research has uncovered a striking number of instances in which Cayce's version of early Christianity echoes published sources from his own time and conflicts with historians' present understanding of the period. *A Dweller on Two Planets* (1899), *The Aquarian Gospel* (1907), *The Oaspe Gospel* (1882), and *The Book of Mormon* all purported to expand the Biblical record of the life of Jesus.[80] Each of these works contains elements that are later found in the Cayce readings; for example, the Akashic records were allegedly the source of *The Aquarian Gospel*.[81] Jesus is named as an Essene in a number of scholarly and popular studies in the eighteenth and nineteenth centuries, as well as in *The Aquarian Gospel,* which like Cayce identifies the Essenes with the Great White Brotherhood.[82] The lost years of Jesus traveling in Asia first appeared in Notovitch's *Unknown Life of*

Jesus Christ (1894), a notorious literary hoax that is echoed by *The Aquarian Gospel.*[83] These and other parallels noted by Bell suggest that the same pattern observed by Lehner in the Egyptian readings is found in the readings on early Christianity. Cayce is found to be more in agreement with previous religious and occult literature than with the consensus of later historians.

     Nevertheless, some of the emphases of Cayce's Christology are harmonious with recent historical reconstructions. In the 1990s, there has been impassioned debate about the historical Jesus, centered on the work of the controversial Jesus Seminar. Among the leading figures in this development is Marcus J. Borg, whose *Meeting Jesus Again for the First Time* asserts that:

1.   The historical Jesus was a *spirit person,* one of those figures in human history with an experiential awareness of the reality of God.
2.   Jesus was a *teacher of wisdom* who regularly used the classic forms of wisdom speech (parables, and memorable short sayings known as aphorisms) to teach a subversive and alternative wisdom.
3.   Jesus was a *social prophet,* similar to the classical prophets of ancient Israel. As such, he criticized the elites (economic, political, and religious) of his time, was an advocate of an alternative social vision, and was often in conflict with authorities.
4.   Jesus was a *movement founder* who brought into being a Jewish renewal or revitalization movement that challenged and shattered the social boundaries of his day.[84]

These affirmations, Borg concludes, are all that can be plausibly asserted of Jesus in light of historical evidence. Cayce's Christology agrees with Borg's in a number of ways. The readings insist on the centrality of Jesus as wayshower for all who seek a closer walk with God. Borg argues for this as the primary implication of research on the historical Jesus. He regards traditional definitions of the Christian life, as either one of belief in particular doctrines or as behavior according to certain moral codes, as inadequate and misleading. Christian life "is ultimately not about believing or being good. Rather . . . it is about a relationship with God that involves us in a journey of transformation."[85] Cayce emphatically supports this perspective, for example in this passage: "Walk with Him! Talk with Him! See *Him* as He manifests in every form of life, for He is Life in *all* its manifestations in the earth!"[86] This view is further expressed in Cayce's exhortation: "Behold, He—the Christ Consciousness—leads, directs; and thou canst rely upon Him, who is able to take thy burdens upon Himself."[87]

Associating with tax collectors and "whores," touching lepers, enjoying public feasts with all manner of companions, Jesus consistently violated purity regulations. Even his calling God by the intimate term "Abba" (more accurately rendered by "Papa" than "Father") is a sign of deliberate flouting of standards of decorum. Several passages in the gospels, for example, "There is nothing from without a man, that entering can defile him: but the things coming out of him, those are they which defile the man,"[88] are taken by Borg as further evidence of this theme. The parable of the Good Samaritan is particularly pointed in its exaltation of compassion over purity rules. The Cayce readings likewise focus on Jesus as one who liberated himself and others from the law:

> He set no rules of appetite. He set no rules of ethics, other than "as ye would that men should do to you, do ye even so to them," and to know "Inasmuch as ye do it unto the least of these, thy brethren, ye do it unto thy Maker." He declared that the kingdom of heaven is within each individual entity's consciousness, to be attained, to be aware of through meditating upon the fact that God is the Father of every soul. . . . Here, then, ye find a friend, a brother, a companion. As He gave, "I call ye not servants, but brethren." For, as many as believe, to them He gives power to become the children of God, the Father, joint heirs with this Jesus, the Christ, in the knowledge and in the awareness of this presence abiding ever with those who set this ideal before them."[89]

Presbyterian theologian Richard Drummond has commended elements of Borg's Christology in his comparative study *A Broader Vision*. Published by the A.R.E. Press, Drummond's book compares Jesus Christ and Gautama Buddha in light of historical scholarship and makes few explicit references to Cayce. The author's affiliation with A.R.E. suggests, however, the organization's sympathetic interest in ongoing scholarly investigations of diverse perspectives on Jesus. As in the case of Atlantis and Egypt, it is unlikely that future research will confirm many of the historical details in the readings. Cayce's general interpretation of Jesus, however, is not out of line with contemporary trends in liberal Protestant theology as exemplified by Marcus Borg.

Plausibilities

In *The Modern Researcher*, Jacques Barzun and Henry Graff provide a useful continuum for the persuasiveness of evidence and arguments. Propositions about history and biography can range from proven to impossible, with intermediate stages of probable, plausible, and possible.[90] In appraising Cayce as clairvoyant historian, it is useful to add the adjectives implausible and improbable to the continuum. Examining the readings' portrayal of history in this light allows for a more nuanced appraisal than a simple true/false dichotomy. There appears to be no case in which historical information in the readings that was not generally known at the time has subsequently been proven true. Increasingly recognized as probable, however, is the influence of Essenes on John the Baptist and Jesus. The Qumran scroll discoveries also tend to confirm Cayce's depiction of women in leadership roles among the Essenes, which had previously been regarded as impossible. It is plausible, according to the work of a few recent geological and Egyptological researchers, that Cayce was correct in claiming the Sphinx to be far older than the generally accepted date, although this continues to be hotly debated. That Plato's legend of Atlantis derives from the existence of some ancient civilization in the Atlantic or elsewhere destroyed by cataclysm is possible, and has given rise to many alternative hypotheses. But a great many of the historical details in the readings are rather implausible, and some are highly improbable. The degree of civilization attributed to Atlantis in the Cayce readings seems much more prophetic of the future than reflective of any past reality. The prevalence of eyewitnesses to the life and death of Jesus among recipients of life readings is so high as to seem implausible to all but extreme admirers. Indeed, the consistency with which people were told that their past lives were intertwined with those attributed to Cayce and his family, in Atlantis, Egypt, Persia, and Palestine, suggests some kind of distortion in the readings. Most of Cayce's descriptions of ancient Egypt remain in the category of extreme improbability according to mainstream scholarship, for example the construction date of the Great Pyramid and all the attendant details of construction. Finally, there are details that are totally impossible: people named Judy and Josie in ancient Galilee; a lifetime on the "coasts of Lorraine," the Atlantean origins of the Mayans, Incas, and Mound Builders, and extreme variations in the human form within the last fifty thousand years.

This range of plausibility indicates that whatever genuine information might have come through Cayce was heavily contaminated with material from unreliable sources. Chief among these seems to be Madame Blavatsky's *The Secret Doctrine*, with its scheme of root-races and great Lemurian and Atlantean civilizations. Cayce appears to have adopted much of the anthropogenesis of Blavatsky without having read her work, which seems most likely to have occurred due to the belief of many of the readings' recipients in Theosophy or its derivatives. Through conversation and correspondence if not through telepathy, Cayce acquired a striking amount of Blavatskianism. Like her, he asserts that human souls descended into bodies that had been gradually evolved for that purpose, and that after this occurrence humans mated with animals, producing viable but monstrous offspring.

David Bell notes that Cayce's depiction of struggle between the "Sons of Belial" and "Sons of the Law of One" echoes themes from several sources; "Sons of Belial" is a Biblical phrase, but "Law of One" is associated with Atlantis in *A Dweller on Two Planets*.[91] Bell associates this theme with the struggle between the Great White Brotherhood and the Brothers of the Shadow in Theosophical lore, or that between the Nephites and Lamanites in the *Book of Mormon*.[92] Like the *Book of Mormon*, Cayce traces the Lost Tribes to the New World.[93] Bell concludes from his study of such evidence, "Although it is true that many themes from the Cayce readings have a venerable history, often reaching back to Plato or the Bible, Cayce's use of them is precisely consistent with the spiritual milieu of his own time *and with no other*."[94] He adds, "Cayce's treatment of Eastern religions and early Christianity clearly reflects the now hopelessly-outdated understanding of his contemporaries, if that . . . "[95]

If many life readings contain descriptions of past lives that are historically implausible, what does this imply about the process by which Cayce acquired the information in the readings? They were produced in an altered state of consciousness following a hypnotic suggestion, usually given by Gertrude Cayce. The form of the suggestion varies slightly, but was usually, "You will give the relation of this entity and the universe, and the universal forces, giving the conditions that are as personalities latent and exhibited in the present life. Also the former appearances in the earth's plane, giving time, place and the name, and that in that life which built or retarded the development of the entity, giving the abilities of the present entity and that [to] which it may attain, and how."[96] Flaws in the details of past lives need not imply that the description of the present personality in a given reading was groundless. Nor does a consistent misreading of one era of history necessarily imply that all the past-life readings are factually unreliable. But there is little evidence, apart from the appreciative remarks of recipients of life readings, to support their historical accuracy. In his dissertation, Harmon Bro notes that some reports in the Cayce correspondence show that people had confirmed their past lives through historical research.[97] But in the absence of details, this claim is impossible to verify. The only book-length investigation into a past life alleged in a Cayce reading is Jeffrey Furst's *The Return of Frances Willard* (1970). A woman called Stephanie in the book had been identified at birth as a reincarnated suffragette and temperance advocate. Employing astrologers, psychometrists, and visits to sites of Willard's career in his investigation, the author concludes that "For Stephanie and myself—our families included—there is no longer any doubt."[98] Furst's evidence for the accuracy of the life readings seems far stronger regarding Cayce's forecasts of Stephanie's life than in any remarkable "hits" concerning Willard. Many people in Cayce's circle came to believe fervently in the life readings, however, and there may be more than subjective validation involved. The readings state that past lives "find expression oft in *feelings* toward places, conditions, individuals . . . "[99] Anecdotal evidence in A.R.E. literature suggests that Cayce did often indicate past lives that were consistent with such feelings on the part of their recipients. One might speculate that he could read the current personality's fascination with medieval France, for example, and unconsciously manufacture a past life to fit that interest. In the case of all the people told they were eyewitnesses to the life of Jesus, there might be a helpful intent to strengthen the spiritual life of Christians behind some unconscious fictionalization.

The most critical examination of Cayce's reliability published under A.R.E. auspices since *The Outer Limits of Edgar Cayce's Power* is found in *Visions and Prophecies for a New Age* by Mark Thurston. He argues that the medical readings establish Cayce as a genuine psychic with "almost undeniable evidence,"[100] but admits that this does not prove life or dream readings to be reliable, nor Cayce's predictions. Thurston suggests that "The past life scenarios of his readings *may* have been only convenient metaphors—much in the way that our dreams provide stories—to communicate perceived patterns of the personality. So at best we can claim that Cayce was in some instances gifted psychically in becoming aware of the mental and emotional makeup of people, whom he often had never met personally. The reincarnation theory itself probably cannot be proved through Cayce's readings."[101]

Cayce stated that all knowledge of past, present and future is "latent within self,—would man but begin to understand."[102] Nevertheless, "It is not meant that information given through this channel should be interpreted as being infallible."[103] It is abundantly evident that the historical information given through Cayce was fallible. He refers to Croesus (the Lydian king defeated by Cyrus the Great) as a Persian ruler,[104] and describes the Talmud as "a combination of the ancient Persian or Chaldean, Egyptian, Indian, Indo-China, and such."[105] One reading states that an entity named Theresa Schwalendahl had lived "on the coasts of Lorraine."[106] Another claims that New Mexican ruins include drawings made ten million years ago.[107]

In response to a question about the accuracy of the readings, Cayce said that they were "Correct in so far as the suggestion is in the proper channel or in accord with the action of the subconscious or soul matter."[108] But what is meant by "the proper channel" for suggestions? In light of the seemingly greater reliability of medical and psychological readings, perhaps clairvoyant time travel was simply not a proper channel for Cayce's abilities. What suggestions were not in accord with Cayce's subconscious or soul matter? It seems that his reading of akashic records was much more useful when dealing with living realities facing people in need of help than in cases involving historical research. The readings explicitly reject the idea that the akashic records exist objectively and independently of human beings: "These records are *not* as pictures on a screen, not as written words, but are as active forces in the life of an entity, and are *often*—as may be sur-mised—*in*describable in words . . . do not make the mistake . . . of at-tempting to discern *spiritual* interpretations with a *material* mind, nor *material* interpretations with the spiritual mind . . . "[109]

The source itself suggests that error creeps in when one takes literally what is in truth symbolic; Cayce's historical information seems to be the aspect of the Cayce readings where this problem is most relevant. Details of past lives may have been simply the means that Cayce symbolized the lessons a counselee needed to master in the present.

The consistency that is taken as a sign of the readings' reliability may actually indicate the reverse. Gina Cerminara states that "One reading never contradicted another, even when a long period of time had elapsed between them. . . . When a group of these readings was compared it was found that all fragmentary details agreed with each other; each reading either repeated part of what had been said else-where, or else added some new detail to the mosaic."[110] This implies, however, that any error, once it was admitted into the world view of the readings, was forevermore enshrined as a permanent dogma. In-consistencies might suggest a self-correcting mechanism at work, but total consistency combined with historical errors indicates a systemic problem. If Theosophical beliefs about Atlantis held by one person receiving a reading were picked up by Cayce telepathically or by normal means, they entered his world view and became groundwork for all subsequent readings. (It should be noted that David Bell identifies certain inconsistencies that challenge Cerminara's assessment, for example, conflicting dates for Cayce's own past life as John Bainbridge, and two counselees told they were the same biblical character.)

Another implausibility related to consistency involves the alleged intertwining past lives of a small number of people through centuries of history. This calls to mind the generally discredited *Lives of Alcyone* by the Theosophist Charles W. Leadbeater. In clairvoyant time travel on a far wider scale than Cayce's, Leadbeater had traced the lives of dozens of prominent Theosophists from the "moon chain" (from which humanity allegedly came to earth) to the present. Time after time, Annie Besant, Leadbeater, Krishnamurti, and their most fervent supporters were allegedly reincarnated in the same times and places. Often they were celebrated historical figures. Leadbeater's biographer Gregory Tillett points out that Ernest Wood, Leadbeater's secretary at the time, later stated that the clairvoyant Theosophist had deliberately concocted past lives in order to flatter or mollify those who wanted to be included in positions of honor in the panorama of Alcyone's trajectory through history.[111] Because Cayce was entranced when giving the readings, deliberate fraud on his part does not seem plausible. (This question is discussed further in chapter 4.) But an unconscious desire to please people by including them in an ongoing historical drama certainly might have been a factor. The readings contain passages in which up to nine current A.R.E. figures are connected in Egyptian past lives. More tellingly, the past lives of others were found quite disproportionately in times and places where Cayce himself had allegedly lived. The standard explanation of this pattern is that people tend to reincarnate in groups, and Cayce's former associates were once more drawn into his life.

Consistency is a factor advanced in favor of claims concerning, for example, UFO abductions. This involves consistency among different witness accounts, which would seem to be an even stronger argument for the validity of their stories than Cayce's consistency is for his version of history. But the lack of corroborating physical evidence suggests another possibility, the presence in the human psyche of certain parallel patterns, called archetypes by Carl Jung. Mark Lehner's comments about the mythic aspects of the Ra Ta story suggest that Cayce's reconstruction of the past may be heavily dependent on archetypal patterns. This does not necessarily imply that there is no valid historical information to be found in the life readings. Possibly, as suggested by Lehner, the ratio of myth to history increases with time elapsed, and recent past lives are the most likely to contain accurate information. The only evidence for reincarnation that has generated widespread serious interest from parapsychologists and scholars is found in the work of Ian Stevenson, whose *20 Cases Suggestive of Reincarnation* remains the best-respected work in the field. All the cases described in the book involve spontaneous memories of very recent past lives by young children, which provided evidence that could be (and was) subsequently checked for accuracy. Hypnotically induced "retrieved memories," beginning with the thoroughly debunked case of "Bridey Murphy," have conveyed subjective certainty to those who experience them and their therapists, without yielding the kind of evidence that makes Stevenson's study impressive. Hypnotic retrieval of memories from childhood is now viewed with increasing skepticism by psychological associations, following a brief period in which it became fashionable and led to obvious abuses. Retrieval of past-life memories is even more problematic from a skeptic's point of view. When, as in the case of Edgar Cayce, the hypnotic subject is not the same person whose past is being retrieved, there is yet another reason to question the validity of the information produced.

For many readers, the most implausible element in the Cayce readings is the belief in reincarnation, rather than any of the specific details about individual past lives. It was shocking to Cayce and his family when past lives began to appear in the readings. Although more than twenty-five percent of Americans currently espouse belief in reincarnation, it is still an obstacle to wider acceptance of the Cayce readings. Paul Edwards, a philosopher, gives Cayce only passing mention in his *Reincarnation: A Critical Examination*. Nevertheless, his book is highly relevant to any evaluation of the Cayce phenomenon. There is much about Edwards's approach that will be offensive to readers sympathetic to Cayce or any form of esotericism, New Age spirituality, or Eastern religion. He engages in extended personal ridicule of his targets, attacks straw men irrelevant to the main theme of his arguments, and makes clear his scorn for any form of religious belief. Despite all this, he raises questions that cannot be ignored by anyone seriously interested in appraising Cayce.

Edwards argues that the form of mind/body dualism on which reincarnation doctrine rests has been increasingly rejected by both science and philosophy. He also observes that the arguments on behalf of reincarnation and karma based on moral necessity lack philosophical clarity and persuasiveness. That is, to use reincarnation and karma in order to retain the idea of a just universe presupposes the assumption that the universe is just, which Edwards regards as untenable. He demolishes several forms of alleged evidence on behalf of reincarnation, simply by showing that such evidence (as in deja vu or child prodigies) can be explained by less extraordinary means.

The book refutes various cases of alleged proof of reincarnation, like that of Bridey Murphy. Edwards explores cases of near-death experiences, citing parapsychologist Susan Blackmore's skeptical dissection of this topic, and analyzing the claims of Elizabeth Kubler-Ross, Raymond Moody, and Stanislav Grof. He attempts to dispose of the doctrine of the astral body as the reincarnating entity, which had been asserted by a few writers. Neither Cayce, Blavatsky and her successors in the Theosophical movement, nor Eastern religions generally teach such a doctrine, so when Edwards asserts triumphantly that the astral body must be as mortal as the physical and cannot therefore reincarnate, he is only echoing the general consensus of esoteric tradition. The term used by Cayce for the reincarnating entity, the causal body, derives from Theosophy and indirectly from Eastern religion, and is alleged to be entirely non-physical.

This raises the philosophical question of the continuity of identity from one life to another. Popular interpretations of reincarnation tend to describe the present identity as being continuous with that of previous lives, and Edwards successfully shows the logical problems of such an approach. In many passages Edgar Cayce seems to endorse such a simplistic identification of past personalities with those of present incarnations. But on closer inspection he, like Blavatsky and most writers on the subject, can be seen to assert something more complex. The simple continuity asserted in popular Western literature echoes popular Hinduism. Buddhism, however, with its "anatman" doctrine, denies that there is any lasting identity in the individual. Comparing rebirth to the lighting of one candle by the flame of another, Buddhism teaches that the seeming continuity from one life to another is that of cause and effect rather than of identity. Thus, one lifetime generates "skandhas" or concatenations of causes which produce effects in future lives. Cayce partially echoes this in his remarks about meeting in the earth the effects of causes sown here, after the disintegration of the constituent parts of the soul during planetary sojourns. Nonetheless, he does assert the reintegration of all of these constituents at the time of rebirth, opening himself to all the philosophical objections against continued identity from one life to another. But the reincarnation doctrine has other forms, to which Edwards's objections on this score are irrelevant.

The most seemingly persuasive argument made by Edwards, in relation to Cayce's version of reincarnation, is based on world population. Citing a study by Arthur H. Westing, Edwards states that there were 200 million humans living at the time of Christ, 500 million in 1650, one billion in 1850, and nearly six billion in the mid-1990s. He concludes that this rules out the claim by Cayce, Blavatsky, and most neo-reincarnationists that human souls can occupy only human bodies and no new "graduates" from animal species have entered the human race in thousands of years.[112] If these numbers are correct, the only way to save belief in reincarnation is to admit the possibility that new souls are created or that animals' souls can graduate to human status. The latter has never ceased to be the position of Hinduism and Buddhism, which account for the vast majority of reincarnationists in the world, so Edwards's argument is less damning than he seems to think. But in any event, a recent article in the A.R.E. publication *The New Millennium* argues persuasively that the demographic "proof" against reincarnation rests on a mathematical error. Eric Youngberg, a graduate student in philosophy at Syracuse University, points out that the most recent estimate is that "99.7 billion people have died in the earth's history."[113] This allows each person now living about nineteen past lives, and demolishes Edwards's demographic argument, which was based on the idea that the majority of people who had ever lived were now alive on earth.

The last two chapters of Edwards's work are the most valuable, in that they critique the most respected body of evidence for reincarnation and assert what Edwards calls the "weightiest argument against reincarnation."[114] The research of Ian Stevenson has been widely acclaimed as the most persuasive case for belief in reincarnation, and Edwards's objections do not disprove that claim. But they do point out weaknesses of methodology and logic that show how far from conclusive Stevenson's findings remain. For Edwards, the strongest argument against reincarnation is the dependence of consciousness on the brain, for which he adduces a growing body of neurological evidence. He acknowledges, however, that the nature of consciousness itself remains a subject of fierce debate among philosophers and scientists. If indeed science and philosophy come to conclusive agreement on this dependence, all forms of belief in after-death survival will be equally at risk, and not just reincarnation.

There is still legitimate scholarly debate about the evidence for and against clairvoyance and telepathy, which together are called General Extrasensory Perception. Those who argue that there is no such thing will of course not consider the possibility that Cayce exemplifies it. On the other hand, if the possibility of GESP is granted, Cayce is one of the most promising case studies for further exploration. Similarly, there is no scholarly agreement on the reality of any form of afterlife, much less the reincarnation hypothesis. None of these issues can be resolved in this book. Neither science nor philosophy can tell us what becomes of us after death, despite the seeming aura of certainty in writings like those of Edwards. Parapsychologists by and large accept the evidence for GESP as persuasive, while avoiding any religious implications thereof. And while the evidence for survival of death can be fairly described as impressive, it is not conclusive. Carl B. Becker, in *Paranormal Experience and Survival of Death*, concludes that survival is "probable" after an extensive survey of the evidence.[115] But it cannot be said to be proven, any more than it can be proven false. In the face of a mystery, religion attempts to provide answers that rest on unprovable assumptions.

Because Edgar Cayce is a case study in parapsychology, and also because his readings were primarily concerned with medical questions, he deserves to be a subject of scientific study. Since his readings recapitulate and synthesize centuries of philosophical doctrines, there is a need for philosophical analysis of his work. But in the final analysis, the most appropriate and promising discipline for Cayce scholarship is religious studies. His life and work touch upon the most profound and elusive mysteries of life and death, and bring together several themes and patterns that have renewed religion in America for the last two centuries. Cayce's role as a prophet of the End Times places him squarely in the tradition of such American religious figures as Joseph Smith and Ellen G. White.

Predicting the Future

The readings contain prophecies dated and undated, with varying degrees of specificity, covering a period from Cayce's lifetime through the year 2158. As a time traveler, Cayce appears to have been more successful in describing the future than the past, with most of his impressive "hits" involving the latter half of the twentieth century. On the other hand, his predictions of events within his own lifetime were particularly fallible. According to Cayce, San Francisco was to have a bigger earthquake in 1936 than in 1906, although by January 1936 he was saying this would not occur.[116] 1934 was foretold to bring a great series of earth changes: "the earth will be broken up in many places ... a change in the physical aspect of the west coast of America ... open waters appear in the northern portions of Greenland ... new lands seen off the Caribbean Sea, and *dry* land will appear ... South America shall be shaken from the uppermost portion to the end."[117] Political predictions for the year were equally dramatic: "There will be the reduction of one risen to power in central Europe to naught. The young king son will soon reign."[118] In response to a question, this country was identified as Germany, and would seem to imply an early end to the Nazi regime and a return of monarchy. 1936 was prophesied to bring severe wars and earthquakes.[119] This would seem to be related to the birth of a divine messenger named John in late 1936, before whose appearance the sun would be darkened and the earth broken up.[120] Upon being asked about the possibility of a second world war, Cayce replied that it was possible but not inevitable, depending on how well international order was reestablished; without world brotherhood, Armageddon would come.[121] Despite the obvious failures of his catastrophic forecasts for the 1930s, there has been continued interest in Cayce's earth change predictions, many of which are not dated so specifically. The best known of these makes a great many startling prophecies:

> In the next few years land will appear in the Atlantic as well as in the Pacific. . . . Portions of the now east coast of New York, or New York City itself, will in the main disappear. This will be another generation, though, here; while the southern portions of Carolina, Georgia—these will disappear. This will be much sooner. The waters of the lakes will empty into the Gulf . . . Los Angeles, San Francisco, most all of these will be among those that will be destroyed before New York even.[122]

As will be discussed below, the end of the period forecast for the inauguration of such extreme changes is approaching. 1998 has great significance in the readings, and is seen as the beginning of a new age of enlightenment and brotherhood. But Cayce saw the end of the second world war as setting the stage for the new order that would gradually emerge:

> Americanism—the ism—with the universal thought that is expressed and manifested in the brotherhood of man into group thought, as expressed by the Masonic Order, will be the eventual rule in the settlement of affairs in the world. Not that the world is to become a Masonic Order, but the principles that are embraced in same will be the basis upon which the new order of peace is to be established in '44 and '45.[123]

1958 is another significant year in the predictions of Edgar Cayce. Physical changes in the Norfolk area would be limited to port improvements and such beneficial man-made changes, beginning "nearer to '58 than to '38 or '36," in a reading that turned out to be quite accurate.[124] Between 1952 and 1964, major tunnel projects were completed linking Norfolk to Portsmouth and Hampton, and connecting the Eastern Shore of Virginia to the mainland. The port of Hampton Roads steadily expanded during the same time period.

Other predictions for 1958 were less successful. Cayce claimed that the "King's Chamber" of the Great Pyramid would be entered between 1938 and 1958, although other predictions gave later dates.[125] Thirty-two tablets from the Tomb of Records were also to be discovered by 1958.[126] One reading predicted that occult forces would be manifested again "in the near future" in the way they had been in the Atlantean period.[127] The meaning of this may be related to another prediction for 1958, that the power to make stones float in the air, used in the construction of the Pyramids, would be rediscovered.[128]

The forty-year period from 1958 to 1998 was predicted to be one of great changes physical and spiritual. The era of transformation "begins in '58 and ends with the changes wrought in the upheavals and the shifting of the poles, as begins then the reign in '98 (as time is counted in the present)."[129] Another passage makes the pole shift seem like a gradual change, saying that it will "begin in those periods in '58 to '98."[130]

A prophecy about the 1960s generated considerable excitement, which waned after further investigation. Poseidia was to rise in 1968 or 1969.[131] Although there was no rising of an island in the Atlantic in those years, another prediction suggests a symbolic interpretation. Cayce said that "a portion of the [Atlantean] temples may yet be discovered, under the slime of ages of sea water—near what is known as Bimini . . ."[132] Although discovery in Bimini of an underwater formation with the appearance of a road excited enthusiasm among Cayce supporters in 1968, the consensus of most researchers has been that the alleged "stones of Atlantis" were of natural rather than man-made origin.[133] Research at this location continues at present.

Cayce's admirers in the 1960s were impressed by his seeming forecasts of the racial strife of that decade. The readings were uncompromising in their view of the need for racial justice: "Who is thy brother? Whoever, wherever he is that bears the imprint of the Maker in the earth, be he black, white, gray or grizzled, be he young, be he Hottentot, or on the throne or in the president's chair."[134] Moreover, Cayce predicted that serious social disturbances would arise if remedial action were not taken, warning that "If those in position to give of their means, their wealth, their education, their position, *do not* take these things into consideration, there must be that leveling that will come. For unless these are considered, there must eventually become a revolution . . . things as crime, riots, and every nature of disturbance."[135] There was no revolution, despite much rhetoric about the possibility, however, and another prophecy seems to have exaggerated the impending disruptions. Cayce warned of a division, a mob rule, "before there is the second of the presidents that next will not live through his office . . . "[136] Since Cayce died before Franklin Roosevelt, this can only be taken to mean that before John Kennedy's death there would be mob rule in America; no events of the period come close to fulfilling this prediction.

On the subject of the future of Russia, however, Cayce was more successful, indicating the downfall of Communist dictatorship:

> In Russia there comes the hope of the world, not as that some-times termed of the Communistic, or the Bolshevistic; no. But freedom, freedom! that each man will live for his fellow man! The principle has been born. It will take years for it to be crys-tallized, but out of Russia comes again the hope of the world. Guided by what? That friendship with the nation that hath even set on its present monetary unit "In God We Trust."[137]

Although the collapse of the Soviet Union gave political and personal freedoms to many within and outside its borders, the new Eastern Europe is not yet a beacon of hope for the world. Friendship with the United States has been an impelling factor in the transformation of the former Soviet bloc, however, and this prophecy by Cayce appeared highly implausible to many until shortly before its fulfillment. His claim that China would become a Christian nation seems implausible, but since no date was given for that prediction, there is perhaps some slight chance of its fulfillment.

The return of Christ figures largely in Cayce's prophecies for 1998 and beyond, which makes his readings particularly interesting at the present time. The readings describe Cayce as a "forerunner of that influence in the earth known as the Christ Consciousness, the coming of that force or power into the earth that has been spoken of through the ages."[138] 1998 was proclaimed as the beginning of a gradual shift into the Aquarian Age, in which Atlantis will rise again.[139] Although the beginning of the Aquarian age is inexact, since astrological eras overlap, "we will begin to understand fully in '98" the implications of the change.[140] In light of the apparent mythical elements in the Cayce readings about Atlantis, it may be plausible to interpret the predicted rise of the lost continent metaphorically. Edgar Evans Cayce describes the readings' Atlantis as "strikingly similar to twentieth-century America."[141] Developments such as laser surgery, atomic energy, domed power plants with the capacity to produce widespread devastation, and advanced agricultural technology all suggest that Cayce's version of Atlantis may have been an unconscious forecast of the future rather than a depiction of the past. Technological advances do feature prominently in the predictive readings. Indeed, Cayce could hardly have been more prescient about life at the end of the twentieth century than in the advice he gave two people in 1944. In March, he counseled one person to begin studying electronics, "For as the earth and the people of same enter Aquarius, the air, we find that the electrical forces, electronics and energies are to be the ruling influences."[142] Three months later, he advised another to "get out of the tobacco business, get into electronics."[143]

The Second Coming and the New Age

There are several levels of interpretation of the Second Coming of Christ given in the readings. Some passages depict the second advent in a traditional mode, for example "He shall come as ye have seen Him go, in the *body* he occupied in Galilee."[144] But other passages suggest a more symbolic interpretation, as in, "He will come again and again in the hearts, the minds, the experiences of those that *love* his coming. But those when they think on him and know what His presence would mean and become fearful, He passeth by."[145] There is no ambiguity, however, in the rejection of a literal reading of the Book of Revelation concerning the Antichrist. Cayce defines it simply as "the spirit of that opposed to the spirit of truth," adding that "The spirit of hate, the anti-Christ, is contention, strife, fault-finding, lovers of praise."[146]

The impulse toward a new spiritual consciousness is predicted to arise in Russia, which will produce "an evolution, or revolution, in the ideas of religious thought . . . not Communism, no!—but rather that which is the basis of same, as Christ taught—His kind of Communism."[147] Equally important to the New Age will be the discovery of ancient records that will confirm the Cayce readings. As mentioned earlier, there is allegedly a "storehouse (where the records are still to be uncovered)" reached by "passage from the right forepaw [of the Sphinx] to the entrance of the record chamber, or record tomb," but these will not be found until "the Fifth root race begins."[148] The term "root race" originates in the Theosophy of H. P. Blavatsky, but according to her doctrines Cayce's prophecy is meaningless, since the fifth root race began a million years ago. Another passage in the readings seems to suggest 1998 as an alternate date of the records discovery which did not occur in 1958, since "The old record in Gizeh is from that as recorded from the journey to the Pyrenees; and to 1998 from the death of the Son of man (as a man)."[149] The journey to the Pyrenees refers to the flight of Atlanteans from Poseidia, with records that eventually reached Giza.

1998 is also foreseen as a key year for a series of dramatic earth changes which will transform the entire earth:

> The earth will be broken up in the western portion of America. The greater portion of Japan must go into the sea. The upper portion of Europe will be changed as in the twinkling of an eye. Land will appear off the east coast of America. There will be the upheavals in the Arctic and in the Antarctic that will make for the eruption of volcanoes in the Torrid areas, and there will be the shifting then of the poles—so that where there has been those of a frigid or the semi-tropical will become the more tropical, and moss and fern will grow. And these will begin in those periods in '58 to '98, when these will be proclaimed as the periods when His light will be seen again in the clouds.[150]

Unless the next two years bring fulfillment of some of these predictions, earth changes will appear to be the least successful aspect of Cayce's clairvoyance. Many other psychics have added to millennial prophecy about earth changes, most notably Annie Kirkwood and Mary Summer Rain. But the A.R.E., despite sponsoring occasional speakers and books on the earth changes theme, takes the definite stance that the predictions in the readings are far from being the most important aspect of the Cayce heritage. Hugh Lynn Cayce took the position that "the effect of the philosophy expressed in the Edgar Cayce readings on individuals is the most valuable part of the work of the Association for Research and Enlightenment."[151]

Martin Ebon's *Prophecy in Our Time*, published in 1968, contains the most balanced evaluation to date of Cayce's prophetic record. Having studied parapsychology for more than a decade, Ebon surveyed a number of possible prophets, and gave Cayce a measured and careful appraisal. Ebon admits disappointment with the sixteen discourses on world and national affairs delivered between 1932 and 1944, which he examined in detail. One "hit" was in 1935, when the readings foretold an alliance between Germany and Japan.[152] But Ebon concludes that most of what Cayce said about European affairs was vague and general, or sometimes dead wrong, as in the case of Adolf Hitler's intentions. He observes that "whatever may have been Cayce's occasionally accurate general predictions, his answers to some specific social questions permitted considerable latitude of interpretation."[153] Ebon regards the health and life readings as "astonishing" and deserving of detailed study.[154] But in the case of the prophetic material (only about two dozen readings), the author concludes that Cayce was acceding to the requests of people who approached the readings as true believers in an all-knowing source, while in fact he was beyond his depth in certain areas.

The appraisal of Cayce as a clairvoyant time traveler is inevitably much less favorable than in regard to the other three roles addressed in this book. It would be unfortunate if his failures in divining the past and future come to overshadow his genuine contributions. For there are many superlatives that can be justly used to describe his place in history. Cayce is, as is often stated, the best-documented psychic who ever lived. He is also the most popular and influential Christian theosopher of the century in the English-speaking world. His impact as a promoter of holistic health ideals and practices places him at the forefront of that movement. Yet the organization devoted to his legacy is firmly committed, at least in theory, to a questioning, objective study of his work. It should not be forgotten that the only book-length study critical of Edgar Cayce's reliability as a clairvoyant was written by his two sons and focused on a number of different areas in which he clearly did not succeed. *The Outer Limits of Edgar Cayce's Power* examines cases like that of the Lindbergh baby, for whom Cayce's readings after the kidnapping are described by them as seeming "completely inaccurate."[155] Of five cases in which a person was dead or dying at the time of the reading, two of these were not recognized by Cayce, which the authors attribute to the nature of the suggestions given. Multiple cases of readings about buried treasure and oil wells are examined as well, none of which was successful. Unlike purely religious organizations, the A.R.E. makes no pretense that the information in the readings is entirely accurate and reliable, promoting an investigative and careful approach to them. Neither Edgar Cayce nor his descendants have been uncritical believers in the readings, and the readings themselves are emphatic in insisting that no one should be. Cayce warned, "But do not let any portion of that published be thrown at the public, or make claims that are not able to be verified from every angle."[156] The recent compilation by Ernest Frejer, *The Edgar Cayce Companion,* is generous in documenting unfulfilled prophecies, and was published by the A.R.E. Press. Such candor is unusual in New Age organizations. One reading stated that "Honest skepticism is a seeker."[157] A goal of this book has been to appraise Edgar Cayce's readings from a standpoint of honest skepticism. Such an approach has been far more welcome in the A.R.E. than would be expected in comparable organizations in the New Age movement. On the other hand, if the A.R.E. is compared to other research organizations rather than esoteric spiritual groups, there is a fair amount of resistance to skeptical perspectives indicated by the books it has published in the past. This, however, appears to be changing.

The New Millennium for December 1996/January 1997 is on the theme of "Ancient Egypt Rising." Although guest editor John Van Auken leans toward accepting Cayce's predictions, a great diversity of points of view is represented. Zahi Hawass is interviewed, Mark Lehner is quoted at length, but Graham Hancock and Robert Bauval are given more attention. The general tone is one of anticipation, but also clear acknowledgment that the 1998 predictions may not be confirmed. This seems typical of the A.R.E. approach to Cayce's accuracy. Different authors have taken widely varying positions on the reliability of Cayce's predictions and retrocognitions. John Van Auken, one of the Executive Directors, has written enthusiastically on the subject, but on the other hand Kevin Todeschi has commented rather skeptically about the earth change prophecies. Harmon Bro writes in his dissertation that the historical information in the readings is highly impressive in terms of authentic names and details[158] and takes the same approach in his Cayce biography. David Bell, who is not an A.R.E. member, has on the other hand suggested the possibility that Cayce's unconscious mind was guilty of searching for answers from "inappropriate sources" and also that his own biases would have filtered the information, especially in the nonmedical readings.[159] In his *Visions and Prophecies for a New Age,* Mark Thurston goes into detail about earth change prophecies that were wrong, and presents four options for dealing with this. The first is to conclude that Cayce had no skills in this area; the second option is that his dates were wrong but not his precognition of events; the third that these prophecies were fulfilled in some symbolic way. The fourth option, which Thurston presents as the most credible, is that people's consciousness changed after the predictions were made, and thus the consequences were different.[160] The problem with this option is that it is precisely that chosen by the UFO cultists described in Festinger's *When Prophecy Fails,* who proclaimed the imminent end of the world in the late 1950s but then took credit for having averted the catastrophe with their prayers. Nevertheless, Thurston has been a

voice of caution on the subject of the prophecies and past-life information in the readings, and this has not prevented him from becoming
an Executive Director of the A.R.E.

The work of Edgar Cayce is better known and more widely
appreciated in the late 1990s than it has ever been. In the summer of
1996, after completing the first draft of this book, I interviewed Charles
Thomas Cayce, president of the Edgar Cayce Foundation, with particular emphasis on the present and future status of scholarship in the
readings and attitudes toward the arrival of 1998.

Dr. Cayce, a Ph.D. child psychologist, lives on a farm in Virginia
Beach with his wife Leslie and their two daughters. His demeanor was
warm, relaxed and open-minded as we discussed the work of his
grandfather and the future of the Cayce legacy. There was no trace of
dogmatism or defensiveness in his responses.

My first question concerned the present status of research in the
readings. Dr. Cayce responded that during a recent A.R.E. tour to
Switzerland he had been favorably impressed with the seriousness of
the scholarship devoted to the legacies of Carl Jung and Rudolf Steiner
in the centers devoted to their work. Although A.R.E. was just beginning to develop along similar lines, Dr. Cayce was enthusiastic about
the potentials for comparable developments in the study of Edgar
Cayce. Recent changes in the management of the A.R.E. had encouraged the development of Atlantic University and the Edgar Cayce
Foundation. The Board of Directors of the A.R.E. was now firmly
supportive of commitment to scholarly investigation of the readings.
The 1995 creation of a four-member Executive Council to replace the
position of A.R.E. President (which Cayce had held in addition to the
directorship of the Edgar Cayce Foundation) was favorable for the
development of the specialized missions of the Foundation and Atlantic University. Atlantic University, which was revived in the 1980s and
now offers an interdisciplinary Master's degree in Transpersonal Studies, was devoted to in-depth comparative analysis of the readings in
relation to other spiritual traditions. Dr. Cayce anticipated cooperation
with visiting scholars who might do research in the readings or super-
vise theses of Atlantic University graduate students. (As of late 1997,
Atlantic University was in the process of becoming independent of the
A.R.E. due to disagreements between the boards of the two organizations. Among the problems was that the A.R.E. board had concluded
that Atlantic University was devoting too little attention to Cayce-
related studies. This suggests that research in the readings may be a
priority for the new institutes to be housed in the building which had
been intended to include A.U.)

Prior to the recent reorganization, the Edgar Cayce Foundation had functioned as a department of the A.R.E. with archival responsibilities. It had maintained contact with recipients of readings and collected source files of articles on Cayce under the direction of Gladys Davis Turner. A major Foundation project was the computerization of the readings. Now that this has been completed, plans focus on building bridges with likeminded organizations devoted to related research, with the objective of reaching a mainstream audience.

Dr. Cayce described one future role of A.R.E. as a bridge-building group networking with various groups in the metaphysical movement. In the past, emphasis had been primarily on outreach to churches, but the current cultural environment allowed for greater openness to nontraditional organizations. He hoped to see greater resources devoted to scholarship in esotericism, and saw the next few years as crucial in defining the roles of Atlantic University, the A.R.E., and the Edgar Cayce Foundation in this direction. He reported that in regard to financial management and Board consensus, the A.R.E. is on firmer footing than at any time since the death of Hugh Lynn Cayce in 1982.

A shift in emphasis was apparent in recent years, Dr. Cayce observed, due to the gradual disappearance of the generation of witnesses to the work of his grandfather. The first half-century of the A.R.E.'s existence had been dominated by people who had known Edgar Cayce and received readings from him. Those who knew and loved him witnessed the skepticism and attacks that greeted his work during his life, and had a cautious, protective attitude as a result. A critical approach to the readings was therefore less likely to find support in the early years than now that a generational threshold had been crossed. I asked about the crucial difference between "testing" the readings and "proving" them; Dr. Cayce responded that the approach of recent members was more objective and critical than in the early years and that therefore "testing" had now superseded "proving" in the organizational mindset. The new generation of members feels appreciative of the readings, and many believe that Cayce's teachings have saved them from ills of spirit, mind, and body. Nevertheless, as the emphasis continues to shift from the person of Edgar Cayce to the principles he espoused, the atmosphere for scholarly study of his legacy grows ever more promising.

One area that seemed particularly relevant to this question was the research at Giza carried out by Mark Lehner. I asked Dr. Cayce about the circumstances surrounding this research, which has recently been the subject of controversial claims in the popular book *The Message of the Sphinx*, by Graham Hancock and Robert Bauval. He explained that the decision to fund carbon dating of the Great Pyramid in the early 1980s had been controversial within A.R.E. circles, and that he himself had been enthusiastic, yet somewhat torn in light of the potential disappointment involved. After discussion within the Board and leadership, it was concluded that testing the validity of the readings was imperative despite the resistance of some segments of the membership. Although Mark Lehner became disillusioned with the historical aspects of the readings, he remained on friendly terms with Dr. Cayce and had never repudiated the spiritual teachings of the readings. Hancock and Bauval have attempted to present Lehner as entirely antagonistic to the Cayce work, but Lehner himself disputes this in an appendix to their book. Dr. Cayce pointed to other examples of objective testing, including Mark Thurston's abovementioned book and several theses written about the readings. The direction of conferences and publications is toward examining evidence pro and con the readings' statements. He felt that the organization was responsible to provide a context for members to evaluate the material.

Asked about the significance of 1998 in the plans of the A.R.E. and its affiliates, Dr. Cayce said that there was no leadership consensus to emphasize strongly the readings' predictions for that year about the Aquarian Age, Second Coming, Hall of Records, and earth changes. However, the membership and reading public are keenly interested in them. Although prophecy is the least understood and shakiest area covered by the readings, he felt it important to discuss these predictions. The sense that civilization is at a crossroads provides a responsibility to address many related issues highlighted in the readings. But Dr. Cayce and the leadership are interested in alternative explanations of the various predictions about the end of millennium, found in only twenty-five readings, and are not committed to a "true believer" insistence on their accuracy.

When asked about the emerging thesis of this book, that the readings' contents were intricately connected to the knowledge and interest of their recipients, more so than to Edgar Cayce's own conscious knowledge or to any absolute source of truth, Dr. Cayce's response was to suggest that this hypothesis could be readily tested by searching the CD-ROM for the appearance of various themes and determining thereby whether they coincide with the appearance of particular individuals receiving readings. Asked whether or not any contrary opinion had ever been expressed about Edgar Cayce's lack of conscious knowledge of most of the subjects addressed in the readings, Dr. Cayce said that his grandfather had read little other than the Bible, but did engage in lengthy correspondence and conversations that might account for his exposure to various themes in the readings' philosophy. Regardless of whatever modification of one's estimation of the readings might result from research along these lines, however, he concluded that the medical readings remain the strongest evidence for the genuineness of Edgar Cayce's paranormal faculties.

Because Dr. Cayce had been trained in clinical psychology, his evaluation of the impact of emphasis on past lives was of particular interest. My experience with the readings and A.R.E. members indicated that the Cayce material was generally helpful to people, but that one exception to this might be the impact of belief in reincarnation. Excessive interest in one's past lives seemed unhealthy and characteristic of the excesses of the New Age milieu, I suggested, and asked his opinion. He replied that he would like to believe that the reincarnation doctrine was more helpful than harmful psychologically, and cited the work of Dr. Brian Weiss, a Miami psychiatrist and bestselling author on past-life memory retrieval, in this direction. But on the other hand, he acknowledged that transference, blame, and projection were all possible unhealthy mechanisms related to belief in past lives, and said his own study group devoted very little time to discussing them. Nevertheless, he concluded, the concepts of the readings, including the medical readings, are intricately connected to belief in reincarnation, and cannot readily be separated from that doctrine.

The stance of the A.R.E. regarding the 1998 prophecies has become more apparent in the year following my interview with Dr. Cayce. The theme of the 1997 Congress was "Preparing the Way," which might seem to suggest feverish expectation. But the welcoming talks given by Charles Thomas Cayce and Mark Thurston were low-key, emphasizing A.R.E.'s long-range plans for the future and the individual's role in spiritual revitalization of the planet. The A.R.E. Board unveiled an ambitious twenty-year plan in 1997, which includes construction of a new facility to house new research institutes. *The New Millennium* took a carefully balanced perspective on the 1998 predictions, giving them in full but including commentary from a variety of sources. Literalism and fundamentalism may be present among some Cayce followers, but are clearly discouraged by the A.R.E. leadership and the Cayce family.

Mark Thurston commented at some length on Cayce's predictions after reading an early draft of the manuscript for this book. His major emphasis was that prophecy is not necessarily the same thing as prediction. "The whole focus of Biblical prophecy is a call to co-create the future responsibly."[161] Thus, Cayce is seen as heir to the Biblical prophets who warned of danger but hoped to prevent future catastrophes by calling humanity to righteousness. Richard Drummond writes that Cayce's "predictions were not of absolutely predetermined events. In the case of warnings they were statements of open-ended trends that were expected to develop in such and such a way unless those concerned changed their minds and ways."[162] This perspective is evident in Thurston's comment that perhaps the Civil Rights movement was instrumental in preventing the kind of mob rule and riots of which Cayce warned. Regarding the misuse of the Blavatskian term "root race," Thurston suggests that Cayce may have perceived a "watershed event—i.e., a dramatically new kind of consciousness arising" and borrowed a Theosophical term to make his point.[163] Citing the case of Jonah and Nineveh, he suggested that "Cayce was trying to fashion himself as that kind of prophet," i.e., one who helps to prevent suffering by warning of dangers ahead.[164] Thurston offered an interesting interpretation of the earth changes predictions: "While not dismissing the possibility of literal earth changes, personally, I think Cayce was visionary in regard to *ecological* catastrophe, but had no good images for this in 1934 or 1941 . . . so 'earthquakes' and 'pole shifts' were the images he saw."[165]

The A.R.E. has never emphasized the historical and predictive elements of the readings as much as their more practical and personal aspects. Thus, in facing 1998, the organization continues its traditional focus on the medical, psychological, and mystical elements of the Cayce legacy.

A 1997 study by Alan Smith of circulation patterns at the A.R.E. Library provides a rough measure of the priority of different subjects among the interests of library users. Since borrowing privileges are included in membership benefits and books are mailed around the world, the statistics reflect the interests of the entire membership rather than just those in the local area. The top fifteen subjects for books circulated in the previous eighteen months were: Edgar Cayce (2,336), Spiritual Life (1,352), Reincarnation (1,274), Meditation (1,134), Mind and Body (1,048), Astrology (912), Dreams (783), Self Realization (762), Psychical Research (700), Healing (693), New Age (690), Alternative Medicine (687), Biography (676), Occult Sciences (667) and Metaphysics (653). Atlantis appears in twenty-ninth place with 479 circulations; Prophecies, with 447, ranks thirty-second; Earth Changes ranks forty-sixth with 379, and Egypt (Antiquities) is fifty-third with 338. (Because most books have more than one subject heading, they can be counted more than once in the totals by category; there were 25,784 "subject uses" compared to 14,607 books circulated.) Smith cautions that the results are somewhat skewed by the subjects that cataloging staff specifically look for when assigning headings, which reflect perceived member interests. But even the cataloging practices of the library provide some indication of organizational attitudes and priorities. Although the Egypt/Atlantis conferences are the best attended of all held at A.R.E., the library figures suggest that historical and prophetic matters are not primary concerns of most members. This indicates that a disappointing 1998 is unlikely to shake member loyalty and support. There seems no danger of a crisis of disillusionment comparable to the Millerites in 1844 or the UFO cultists of the 1950s.

In the July/August 1997 issue of *Venture Inward*, editor A. Robert Smith comments on the possibility of disappointed expectations:

> Many tend to believe that something quite momentous is immi-
> nent because of statements in the readings. . . . But what if none
> of this happens? Such an eventuality would be devastating to a
> cult. For us, however, it should occasion only deeper reflection,
> seeking ultimate answers not from yesteryear's revealed wisdom
> for our predecessors, but from continuing revelation that is open
> to each of us today, tomorrow, and eternally, if only we will
> venture inward.[166]

With its focus on "turning stumbling blocks into stepping stones," the A.R.E. seems well prepared to survive any disappointment that failed prophecies might bring. In the following issue of *Venture Inward*, however, there was a report that encouraged those who hope for fulfillment of Cayce prophecies about 1998. A.R.E. member Joseph Schor headed a research expedition to Egypt in April 1996, searching for the Hall of Records that Cayce had said would be discovered in 1998. The expedition, affiliated with Florida State University, used radar to search for underground anomalies near the Sphinx. At the 1997 annual A.R.E. conference on Atlantis and Egypt, Schor announced "We've found a room that is about twenty-five feet by forty feet. The walls are parallel. The roof is about thirty-five feet below ground. We don't know where the ground [floor] is, but we think it is sixty to eighty feet below the surface."[167]

Zahi Hawass, director of the Giza pyramids, also spoke at the conference, urging caution. He suggested that the radar could be showing a natural chasm rather than a man-made room, and pointed out that radar used in such a manner has not been proven accurate. Schor and Hawass both agreed that excavation under the Sphinx is impossible due to the fragility of the monument. Schor, however, reported that a shaft leading to the underground room from a point only six feet below the surface had been located, and it could be opened without drilling. Government permission to explore the shaft awaits second and third opinions from reputable sources concerning the radar results. A.R.E. Executive Director John Van Auken reported that he was working with Schor to obtain expert opinions that could be forwarded to Hawass and his colleagues.[168]

Schor's search for the Hall of Records was inspired by Cayce's predictions, so if something is indeed discovered there it might be argued that the prophecy was self-fulfilling. The wait for further evidence will make 1998 a year of anticipation for A.R.E. members and Cayce admirers. Confirmed discovery of an underground chamber near the Sphinx would indeed be a fairly impressive "hit" for Cayce's predictive abilities, even granting a self-fulfilling element. But far more startling would be the discovery of 13,000-year-old records there, and most astonishing of all would be evidence supporting Cayce's descriptions of ancient Egypt and Atlantean migration. No such eventuality is mentioned in the *Venture Inward* report of the Schor expedition, which indicates that A.R.E. leadership is determined to steer clear of potentially embarrassing claims about prophecy fulfillment as 1998 approaches.

4.1

Edgar Cayce, circa 1940.

4

Esoteric Psychologist

The Cayce readings address a wide range of psychological issues of concern to twentieth-century readers. Their approach to such issues frequently parallels those found in ancient and modern esoteric systems. Cayce was not an esotericist in the popular sense of the word, i.e., a teacher of secret lore reserved for initiates. But his explanation of the human soul and its place in the cosmos reverberates with echoes of esotericism as defined in academic studies. This definition focuses on characteristic themes appearing consistently in a wide variety of Western sources, including Gnosticism, Kabbalah, Hermeticism, and Rosicrucianism. Antoine Faivre suggests four essential components of esoteric thought: correspondences, living nature, imagination and mediations, and the experience of transmutation.[1] Each of these is found in the Cayce readings, particularly in their psychological doctrines.

A personality theory of surprising subtlety and complexity emerges from the thousands of life readings. The dream interpretations and theories about dreaming in the readings are among the most compelling aspects of Cayce's legacy, and are rather reminiscent of Jungian psychology, but also chart aspects of dream interpretation ignored or minimized by Jung. Attitudes and emotions as explained in the readings are harmonious with contemporary therapeutic approaches. But Cayce's psychological insights have more in common with a number of systems, Western and Eastern, derived from esotericism. The readings' discussion of reincarnation and karma is reminiscent of the Theosophy of H. P. Blavatsky. Astrological theories enunciated by Cayce are a unique combination of ancient mysteries and contemporary criticism. The group work and discipline encouraged in the readings have practical links to the Fourth Way teachings of George Ivanovitch Gurdjieff and his disciple Peter Demian Ouspensky. Meditation practices taught in the readings have more in common with the nineteenth-century Hindu movement known as Radhasoami than any other known source. Cayce's replies to questions about paranormal faculties and their limitations yield a parapsychological paradigm that combines esoteric tradition with depth psychology. Although the readings are in themselves neither systematic nor scholarly in their approach to psychological questions, they provide rich source material for study of both esotericism and psychology, and a holistic approach that makes them timely a half-century after Cayce's death.

Spirit, Mind, and Body

The triune nature of the self is often repeated in the readings; this is often summarized as "the Spirit is the Life, Mind is the Builder, the Physical is the result," although that precise formula is not found in the readings. Spirit is the universal life, synonymous with Creative Forces or God, and overshadowing all living beings: "one finds self as a shadow, or as a representative of that indicated in the eternal . . . it is time, space and patience that bridges the distance."[2] Time, space, and patience are the second key triad in Caycean psychology, defining the circumstances in which the spirit is individualized and expressed in material form. The readings often use the terminology "spiritual body, mental body, and physical body,"[3] somewhat reminiscent of Theosophical references to "astral" and "causal" bodies that coexist with the physical. In both systems there are said to be bodies that survive physical death, in which are stored the elements of lasting identity. Defining the "life or spiritual or creative forces" as positive and the "body forces in material manifestation" as negative, Cayce recommended, "to reach that as to where they will not be as combative forces is to unify the purposes, the energies, the activities."[4] The keynote of Cayce's psychological approach is that "there must be considered the self as an entity, an integral factor in the seeking to know that as goes on from within and without."[5]

Mind is constantly identified as the Builder, the "active principle that governs man," the principle that intervenes between the spirit, soul, and body. The conscious mind "is able to be manifested in the physical plane through one of the senses," while the subconscious mind lies "between the soul and spirit forces."[6] The will is described as the opposing principle to mind, since mind tends to operate by habit and an act of will goes against that habitual grain. When the personality is governed by the unenlightened will, the result is selfishness. The readings comment: "What is ever the worst fault of each soul? *Self—self!* What is the meaning of self? That the hurts, the hindrances are hurts to the self-consciousness; and these create what?

Disturbing forces, and these bring about confusions and faults of every nature."[7]

Mind is "both spiritual and physical," with lower life forms having "Group Mind" while humans have individual free will.[8] The spirit is like a guardian angel "ever before the face of the Father, through same may that influence ever speak– but only by the command of or attunement to that which is thy ideal."[9] Although spirit and matter are both described as substances in the readings, mind is conceived as a dynamic process that relates the spiritual and the material. Mind is called a "stylus" the activities of which make a "record upon space and time" for each entity.[10] Cayce describes mind as "an active force that partakes of spiritual as well as material import . . . an essence or flow between spirit and that which is made manifest materially."[11] In two passages, the readings use the symbol of a stream to characterize the mind's function: "Mind is a stream, not mind as purely physical or as wholly spiritual, but is that which shapes, which forms, which controls . . . "[12] and "Mind, then, becomes as a stream, with its upper and lower stratum, with that which moves swiftly or that which is resting upon either spirit or physical being."[13] Cayce provides another triune model to explain the operation of the mind, using terminology familiar from analytic psychology. Although, in one reading, Cayce advised that Blumenthal "Study Freud, study astrological aspects, study numerology"[14] as means of understanding personality, his approach has more in common with Jung than with Freud. The soul is equated in the readings with the "spiritual body," which consists of spirit, mind, and will. Psychologist and A.R.E. author Herbert Puryear comments that the spiritual body "carries the record of all thoughts and activities of its individual experience" and is "an energy pattern which carries information."[15] Its origin and destiny, and therefore its essence, is one with God. Cayce refers to the soul as the "inmost self," which brings to mind Jung's suggestion that "the total personality which, though present, cannot be fully known" be called the "self."[16]

According to the Cayce readings, the mind is both the "personality and individuality of an entity" with two phases, one "builded for the development of the soul body," which is "for the expression of the soul mind, or superconscious mind."[17] This higher aspect of the mind becomes increasingly dominant as the soul develops; as "the less and less of self is expressed and more and more . . . the attributes of the soul-body."[18] Individuality is the "inner self," which is "deep, far reaching" and of which we become aware only gradually: "Know that in patience ye become aware of thy soul. And thy body and thy mind, and thy soul, are one. They live together. Your personality, then, is the material expression; and your individuality is the personality of the soul."[19] Personality is "that seen by others," while individuality is "that which shines out from within."[20] Individuality arises from ideals, whereas personality arises from urges.[21] These definitions of individuality and personality are comparable to those presented by Gurdjieff for "essence and personality": "Essence is I—it is our heredity, type, character, nature. Personality is an accidental thing—upbringing, education, points of view—everything external."[22] Gurdjieff's terminology builds upon Theosophical distinctions between personality and individuality, but Cayce's model of the self also incorporates the terminology of analytic psychology. The readings define the conscious mind as "*that* that is able to be manifested in the physical plane through one of the senses," while the subconscious mind is "That lying between the soul and spirit forces within the entity . . . Unconscious force . . . "[23] Superconscious mind is "that of the spiritual entity . . . a portion of the great Universal Forces."[24] The subconscious is identified as a storehouse of memory.[25] Just as the body is fed by physical food, the mind is fed by mental nourishment: "[T]he body-physical becomes that which it assimilates from material nature. The body-mental becomes that it assimilates from both the physical-mental and the spiritual-mental. The soul is *all* of that the entity is, has been or may be."[26] One may make a rough equivalence between the mental body and the conscious mind, the spiritual-mental and the superconscious, and the physical-mental and the subconscious. The goal of the readings' counsel is to align and harmonize the three. Balance is always emphasized, the ideal being "to keep the mental and physical and spiritual body as one, or properly balanced in its relationships to all phases."[27] There is frequent stress on positive thinking in the readings, for "unless the activities, the thoughts are CONTINUOUSLY constructive, and the experience well-balanced, the entity CANNOT, WILL not fulfill the purpose for which it came into the present experience."[28] Acceptance of conditions as they are presented will ensure that they "enlighten the body-mind" so that whatever is necessary for development will occur.[29]

Although the readings emphasize positive thinking, they do not encourage unrealistic optimism. Individuals are advised to recognize their own responsibility for difficulties in relationships, "For each soul, each entity, *constantly* meets self. And if each soul would but understand, those hardships which are accredited much to others are caused most by self. *Know* that in those you are meeting *thyself!*"[30] This echoes the Jungian idea of individuation, as well as the need to integrate the "shadow" rather than project it onto others. The shadow, according to

Jung, is the "dark characteristics" which "have an *emotional* nature, a kind of autonomy, and accordingly an obsessive or, better, possessive quality."[31] Effort and insight are required to integrate the shadow into the conscious personality, and some aspects are especially resistant; Jung writes that "These resistances are usually bound up with *projec-tions*, which are not recognized as such . . . "[32] Projection, a defense mechanism that denies darker elements of the personality and per-ceives them instead only in others, is implied by this passage from the readings: "That one cannot endure within itself it finds as a fault in others."[33] The therapeutic advice found in the readings is, however, quite different from that of any form of analytic psychology. The per-sonal growth techniques most strongly recommended by the readings are: setting ideals and trying to harmonize one's life with them, using astrological insights to understand one's karma, practicing medita-tion, recording and studying dreams, making a commitment to serve others, and gradually unfolding one's psychic sensitivity.

Ideals are a crucial element in Cayce's spiritual psychology. He strongly urges that people write down their spiritual, mental, and physical ideals.[34] Then all decisions may be evaluated in terms of their harmony with the stated ideals, which may and indeed must be changed from time to time. The readings state that "the will, the de-sire, and that which the self sets as the ideal—whether pertaining to the material, the mental or the spiritual forces—should be the guide . . . "[35] By focusing always on one's highest ideal, one banishes fear, for, "Keep thine face toward the light, and the shadows will not bring fright . . . "[36] Ideals provide a means of strengthening the will and promoting greater self-awareness. According to the readings, whenever choices are made consciously, the will is active, but "When this is not in action, then the environmental sphere has its sway."[37] Only self-observation can enable one to recognize how often we are not in control of our own choices. Cayce's phrase for self-observation is "standing aside and watching yourself go by."[38] This prescription is an essential part of the esoteric psychology of Gurdjieff, who taught that "As long as a man does not separate himself from himself he can achieve nothing, and no one can help him."[39] Several of the goals of self-observation in Gurdjieff's system are also emphasized in the Cayce readings. Replacing "internal considering" with "external consider-ing" in the Gurdjieff Work means to focus one's awareness more on the experience of others than oneself. The readings state that "unless one is as considerate of others as there is the desire for others to be considerate of self . . . there come turmoils and strifes."[40] Another ele-ment of the Gurdjieff teachings which resonates with the readings is his distinction between the Law of Accident and the Law of Fate. This holds that individuals can by their own choice determine which of two laws governs their existence. Under the Law of Accident, events are random and have no individual meaning; according to Gurdjieff, if one lives according to this assumption, it becomes a self-fulfilling prophecy. One does experience life as a series of random events without individual meaning. But under the Law of Fate, all events are profoundly meaningful and directly fated for the evolution of the individual. One who perceives and interprets life according to this principle will find it confirmed by experience. Cayce's parallel doctrine is that "Until individuals are in their thought, purpose and intent the law—that is constructive—they are subject to same."[41] Here the description is of a single law to which humans can be subject, but which can be transcended through a constructive attitude. Gurdjieff is also, in essence, describing a single law from two polarized perspectives. "Locus of control" is the psychological term for this difference of perspective. One with an outer locus of control experiences events and indeed laws as controlled by others or by chance. An inner locus of control equates to "becoming the law" inasmuch as one perceives oneself as being ultimately in control of one's life. One of the evaluation measures for a readings-based A.R.E. cassette program on transforming attitudes and emotions is a questionnaire on locus of control. After completion, participants have been found generally to perceive less control from powerful others or chance, and more control from within or from Universal Forces. This makes for greater psychological well-being due, perhaps, to the effects of a constructive attitude.

The readings are quite unusual for their time in their nonjudgmental tone regarding sexual relationships. Upon being asked about non-marital sex, Cayce said it was "a matter of principle within the individual" and that "The sex organs, the sex demands of every individual, must be gratified in *some* manner as a portion of the biological urge within the individual."[42] Even more avant-garde was the statement that nudism likewise was a matter of individual choice and not one of moral principle.[43] Yet the readings also advised that sexual awakening "must be a stepping-stone for the greater awakening," rather than simply a source of physical gratification.[44] The first requirement for any sexual expression would then be that it accord with one's ideals spiritually, mentally, and physically. Cayce, both in the readings and in correspondence, expressed an understanding of sexuality that was liberal for his time. His readings and letters to a young homosexual man who was tormented by his orientation are noteworthy in this regard. He wrote, for example, "That your experience has brought you manifestations that have at times, or often, expressed themselves in sex is not be wondered at, when we realize that that is the expression of creative life on earth. But if we lose sight that it is an expression of God and accredit it to something else, we deny the very promises He has made us all."[45] Cayce further encouraged the young man to have an active social life.

The similarities between the readings and various psychological systems extant during Cayce's life do not seem to be attributable to any conscious understanding of those systems on his part. Freud is mentioned in seven documents, but only one was in a reading, which recommended studying him. In *A Seer Out of Season*, Harmon Bro notes that in 1901, the year Cayce gave his first reading, Freud published *The Interpretation of Dreams*, and James was giving his lectures which became *The Varieties of Religious Experience*.[46] James was also later recommended for study in the readings, but neither the readings nor Cayce's published lectures give much evidence of his understanding James or Freud. The case of Jung is similar, in that he is rarely mentioned on the CD-ROM and never in a reading. Gina Cerminara, a Ph.D. in psychology, used Jungian ideas as parallels to the readings, but like Bro she concluded that "it is unlikely that Cayce even knew who Jung was, let alone his ideas."[47] In fact Cayce received three letters mentioning Jung, but these said nothing about the ideas of the Swiss psychoanalyst. Cayce incorporates belief in God and the paranormal into his psychology, whereas Jung is much more ambiguous on their objective reality. David Bell points out relevant differences between "meeting self" and integrating the shadow, the former implying that our choices create karma, the latter that aspects of the psyche rejected by the conscious mind shape the unconscious and give rise to projection.[48] Nevertheless, Cayce does describe projection in his own terminology, as seen above. Cayce's understanding of dreams is much more religious than Jung's, being influenced by the Bible, but the "patterns" he discerns in dreams are similar to Jungian archetypes. The readings' distinction between personality and individuality is as akin to that proposed by Theosophy in the nineteenth century as to Jung's later formulation. Jung was not well known in the United States during Cayce's lifetime. Some central Jungian notions are not found in Cayce, but there is agreement in the role of dreams as a gateway to a realm of meaning that is transpersonal in nature. Less evident in the readings are such Jungian ideas as individuation, the four functions, and alchemical symbolism. A.R.E. writers after Cayce, however, have been quite interested in Jung. Harmon Bro practiced Jungian psychotherapy and explored reincarnation with clients years after his work with Cayce, and uses Jungian terms liberally in his dissertation.[49] Mark Thurston has also stressed similarities between the Jungian and Caycean approaches, and as discussed in chapter 3, Charles Thomas Cayce regards cooperative ventures with Jungians as a positive future direction for the Edgar Cayce Foundation.

Parallels to the Gurdjieff system are even more tenuous from the point of view of historical evidence. Gurdjieff himself is never mentioned in the readings, although Ouspensky appears several times. His *Tertium Organum* is among the books recommended for study by the readings, but it precedes Ouspensky's Gurdjieff involvement by several years, being written during his earlier Theosophical phase. One of the oddest elements of this puzzle is that Ouspensky is cited as a source of channeled messages in an early reading for Morton Blumenthal's wife ("Ouspensky giving this"), despite the fact that he was alive at the time.[50] A 1943 reading answered a question posed by a sixty-eight-year-old woman about returning to her study with Ouspensky in New York, but this is the only indication of Cayce's counseling Fourth Way disciples. Although self-observation is recommended by both Cayce and Gurdjieff, the latter is much more focused on independence, whereas Cayce analyzes choice in terms of harmony with God's will. "Law of . . . " terminology is found in New Thought literature of the nineteenth century, so that parallel between Cayce and Gurdjieff may also be coincidental. Gurdjieff has definitely had some posthumous influence on the A.R.E., however, through Mark Thurston's companion volumes to the *Search for God* texts, which prescribe exercises modeled somewhat on Fourth Way prototypes. All of the abovementioned psychological systems contain striking parallels to the Cayce readings, but evidence of historical influence is very weak. The same pattern is apparent in the meditation guidelines given by the readings, as seen below. As a general rule, the Caycean psychological material has less obvious relationship to environmental influences than his medical, religious, and historical information. For many observers it is the most valuable and compelling aspect of the readings.

In his dissertation and biography, Harmon Bro emphasizes that Cayce's authority was "that of a religious counselor, one who was expected to help people on whatever level they sought help—medical, vocational, psychological—but through all quietly to urge them to take account of God's care for them and demands upon them."[51] To call Cayce an esoteric psychologist implies more than simply that he presented a system of psychological ideas. He was also a counselor and even in a sense a therapist. Bro observes: "He made it a point to get acquainted with the counselees, either before or after he gave them readings . . . he could give a better reading, one with more detail and clarity of expression for the person under consideration, if he got the feel of the man and the man got his feel and trusted him—tried to 'tune in' to him."[52] The plea to the angelic being of his childhood that he be enabled to help others resonates for Bro as the keynote of Cayce's readings: "His deepest promise, which he saw as the ground of his ability, had been to lift pain from sufferers."[53] Because immediate one-to-one counsel was the heart of Cayce's life work, Bro warns against the danger of "viewing Cayce as a purveyor of unusual data or teachings rather than as a channel of active love, deftly and incisively varying his aid from person to person."[54] The two most common responses of readings recipients are given by Bro in the words he heard from individuals at the time their readings were received: "We are known, all the way. And not just by Cayce," and, "How we are loved!"[55] The charisma of Edgar Cayce rested, according to Bro, precisely in his ability to convey this sense of reassurance to troubled souls: "His concern was not first of all with powers but with relationships . . . he sought to be deeply and helpfully related to the damaged persons that he served."[56] His degree of skill in readings was proportional, in Bro's observation, to the counselee's "ability to act productively on what he supplied."[57] This might be said of any counselor, and places Cayce in a different category from prophets whose message is to collectivities rather than individuals. The primary theme of Bro's dissertation is that Cayce's charisma can best be understood as that of seership, which he defines according to the phenomenological description offered by Wach, whose typology of religious authority-bearers places seers in a position inferior to prophets due to their relative passivity. Seers use intuitive or visionary processes to respond to individual questions or problems, whereas prophets speak to collective needs and appeal to group identity.[58] The seer's gift is exclusively cognitive in nature; he cannot work wonders or convey blessings.[59] Bro portrays the seer as having authority and power due to "archetypal profundity and striking psi-cognition" but as being stunted by the inability to "demonstrate other gifts beyond cognition."[60] Only Andrew Jackson Davis and Emanuel Swedenborg in modern Western history are comparable to Cayce as examples of seership, in Bro's estimation.[61]

Any scientific explanation of Cayce's readings must rest on an understanding of trance, yet the Unconscious in the traditional sense has never been accepted as a scientific concept. Relying on Jungian or Freudian categories to explain Cayce invites rejection from readers who dismiss such categories as "occult" rather than scientific. In the years when behaviorism was the dominant paradigm, all talk of the

Unconscious was dismissed, and only gradually has the concept acquired a certain legitimacy in experimental psychology. Although any
explanation of Cayce is subject to revision as psychology advances,
some recent progress in research helps to suggest fruitful avenues of
inquiry. In *The Emotional Brain,* Joseph LeDoux provides a summary of
recent psychological and neurological research on emotion. The Unconscious of Jung and Freud has never been accepted by experimental
psychology or neurology, but there is currently a trend toward acceptance of the "emotional unconscious" and "cognitive unconscious."

Coined by psychologist John Kihlstrom, the term "cognitive unconscious" refers to all the cognitive processes that occur without consciousness. The field of cognitive psychology has made significant strides
toward understanding the way information is processed by the brain,
which is almost entirely unconscious. Using the metaphor of computer
problem solving, cognitive psychology avoids conceptualizing the unconscious as a dynamic motivating factor in behavior, as it has been
portrayed by Freud, Jung, and Cayce. But as the study of emotions and
neurology proceeds, there is increasingly strong evidence for unconscious processing of emotions. LeDoux uses the term "emotional unconscious" to refer to these processes, and cites conclusive studies to justify
acceptance of the term, anathema to the behaviorist orthodoxy that
dominated the field until recent years. Cognition and emotion are both
readily discernible in a great variety of animal species, whereas consciousness appears to be limited to humans and higher primates.[62]

Dividing the unconscious into cognitive and emotional processes
is helpful in understanding the varying reliability of different categories of readings. If Cayce was indeed capable of attuning himself to
the unconscious of the person for whom he did the reading, as many
recipients believed, current terminology would suggest two comple-
mentary aspects of this ability. His empathic communication with the
emotional unconscious would manifest in readings that interpreted
dreams (which may also reveal the cognitive unconscious) or described
life issues facing the subject. Medical readings also often included
commentary on emotions. But when Cayce attuned himself to the
cognitive unconscious, he spoke in the language of the belief system
of the person for whom he did the reading. Thus the prevalence of
Protestants, Spiritualists, New Thought followers, and Theosophists
among readings recipients would ensure that these groups' doctrines
were reflected in the world view emerging through Cayce, with his
own religious background supplying the basic "grammar," to use
Prothero's metaphor. The margin of error in this aspect of Cayce's
readings would therefore be considerably greater, as there is far more

consistency in people's emotional processes than there is in their thinking. Similarly, with medical readings, people's bodies are far more similar than their ideas about religion or history, so the likelihood of Cayce's access to objective truth is greater.

Astrology

Reincarnation may be the best-known element of the life readings; thousands of past lives are described in them, ranging from Atlantis to nineteenth-century America. The readings themselves state that the fact of reincarnation "needs stressing to answer many questions."[63] Chapter 3 examines these readings along with those that portray the future clairvoyantly. But the process of reincarnation is only half of the explanation of after-death states found in the readings. What occurs between incarnations is also explained in considerable detail, providing a new interpretation of astrology. The readings teach that at least thirty incarnations are necessary before one can reach a level of perfection enabling one to move to another stage of soul expression.[64] Asked about the "law of relativity," Cayce replied that the soul is developing to become one with God, which requires passage through "all the planes in the universal forces," meaning that each is in a "relative condition, position, action, state of being, to that creative force, and that created."[65] Our passage through "all the planes" involves what the readings call planetary sojourns. "What we create in the earth we meet in the earth—and what we create in the realm through spiritual forces we meet there."[66] The realm to which this refers is the solar system, and the readings repeatedly describe sojourns of the discarnate soul on the planets. It is not entirely clear what relationship the planets bear to the interlife experience, but each planet is said to "represent as it were one of the phases of our conscience—the elements of our understanding—or our senses," implying that "they each in their place, in their plane, bear a relationship to us . . . "[67] In another reading, the interlife sojourns are called "stages of consciousness; given names that represent planets or centers of crystallized activity."[68] Cayce summarized the meanings of the sojourns:

As in Mercury pertaining of Mind. In Mars of Madness. In Earth as of Flesh. In Venus as Love. In Jupiter as strength, in Saturn as the beginning of earthly woes, that to which all insufficient matter is cast for the beginning. In Uranus as of the Psychic. In that of Neptune as of Mystic. In Septimus as of Consciousness. In Arcturus as of the Developing.[69]

These correspond approximately to the meanings attributed to the planets in traditional Western astrology, with the exception that Arcturus, a star, is identified by Cayce as a way station through which souls enter and exit the solar system. There are other inhabited solar systems in the universe, according to the readings.[70] Beginning in 1923, the readings refer to a planet called Septimus, which after the discovery of Pluto was called by that name. Each sojourn is in a state of consciousness that can be associated with one of the planets, but does not involve incarnation: "Not that ye maintain a physical earth-body in Mercury, Venus, Jupiter, Uranus or Saturn, but there is an awareness or a consciousness in those realms when absent from the body, and the response to the position those planets occupy in this solar system."[71] This is part of a natural process whereby the soul entity is broken up into constituent elements. These constituents are correlated with the planets, but also with different mathematical dimensions: "not only three dimensions—as of the earth—but there may be as seven, in Mercury—or four, in Venus—or five, as in Jupiter . . . only one as in Mars . . . many more as in those of Neptune, or they may become even as nil—until purified in Saturn's fires."[72] These dimensions, according to another reading, are "not as of planes, as sometimes spoken of, but consciousnesses . . . "[73] These consciousnesses can be equated with the pagan gods whose names have been given to the planets, although they are mere instruments of the one God: "those that speak of the *gods* of the universe are proper in their concept, *would* they be *considered* as an *individual* division of the various spheres—but *God,* in His heavens, the Maker of ALL, is as the ONE GOD, the ONE source!"[74]

A natal chart is, according to the readings, a reflection of the results of one's planetary sojourns. The natal positions of the planets are thus said to be effects or indicators, rather than causes, of personality traits. Influences from the sojourns play a different role than those from past earth-lives. The former are said to "manifest in the experience of self through the innate or the deeper mental self."[75] This can be equated with "the intuitive response of the inner self *to* outside influences, while the material sojourns make up the emotional self, or the self that responds through the emotions of the body as arise from associations of same."[76] Karma associated with the physical body, including emotions, is made up of past earth-life tendencies, whereas intellectual and spiritual qualities derive from the planetary sojourns. In another reading, the distinction is reiterated: "sojourns in the earth . . . [are] indicated in the emotions, while the astrological sojourns manifest an awareness in the mental thinking, or the manner of thinking, or the manner of approach from the spiritual through the mental to the material."[77] The nearly equal emphasis given in the readings to past lives and planetary sojourns suggests their influence to be of approximately equal importance. In some unexplained manner, the planetary and earthly influences are registered in the seven energy centers or chakras, called in the readings "phases of experience and of reactions of sojourns of the entity."[78]

The doctrine that souls pass through the spheres of the solar system between earth-lives is of ancient origin. Found both in Greek and Iranian traditions, it has not been fully expounded in either, perhaps due to its relation to the mysteries. The most explicit formulation of the doctrine in modern occultism is found in the work of Gottfried de Purucker, Leader of the Theosophical Society—Point Loma. Purucker speaks of the planetary sojourns as "outer rounds": "The Spiritual Monad or Ego it is which peregrinates on the Outer Rounds, that is, from planet to planet, or more accurately from planetary chain to planetary chain."[79] In his system, the soul also migrates through the "earth chain," a set of globes of varying degrees of materiality.

The Cayce readings acknowledge certain problems with Western astrology as presently practiced. The precession of the equinoxes makes the tropical zodiac anachronistic, as "most astrologers are nearly thirty degrees off in their reckoning in the present."[80] This is not as damaging to Caycean astrology as to the mainstream approach, since the readings place overwhelming emphasis on planetary influence rather than that of signs or houses. Indeed, the parallels between Cayce and traditional astrology are few. Margaret Gammon explains the results of research into the charts of persons who had received life readings, concluding that "A study of the most important planets mentioned in 150 children's readings shows that it is more than likely that there will be no orthodox astrological aspects between them . . ."[81]

The readings are more aligned with tradition in their interpretation of transiting aspects, presenting trines as favorable and squares as unfavorable. But by and large, Cayce affirms astrology in principle while differing with its current practice. It is therefore interesting that the sole astrological researchers whose solid results are most widely hailed point to the same planetary emphasis as found in the Cayce readings. Michel and Francoise Gauquelin had only negative results when seeking correlations between signs or houses and personality traits. But when they studied the planets in positions near the angles of the charts in a series of celebrities, they found statistically meaningful patterns. Mars in such a position correlates with military careers; the Moon is found near angles in charts of writers; Saturn is correlated with charts of political figures; and so on. There has been no credible challenge to the findings of the Gauquelins. In the most thorough scholarly study of astrology to date, Hans Eysenck and D. K. B. Nias report that "The work of the Gauquelins . . . stands up to a careful degree of scrutiny, and compares favorably with the best that has been done in psychology, psychiatry, sociology, or any of the social sciences."[82] The authors add that they can find "no valid major criticism of their conclusions, methods, or statistics."[83] They conclude that "The curious relationship between Gauquelin's findings of planetary association with prominence in different occupations, and the astrological symbolism of the planets concerned"[84] remains the strongest evidence yet marshaled on astrology's behalf.

In their astrological emphasis, the Cayce readings have more in common with the teachings of two twentieth-century successors to Blavatsky than with the original Theosophical doctrines. Rudolf Steiner and Alice Bailey were both highly visible, active Theosophists prior to breaking with the leadership of the Theosophical Society. Steiner and Bailey were contemporaries of Edgar Cayce, and like him they adapted Blavatsky's esoteric synthesis in a Christian setting, and emphasized occult interpretations of the second coming of Christ. Steiner, like Cayce, sees the Christ as the central figure in human history; he identifies 1998 as the climax of a conflict between Christ and Antichrist.[85] The modern A.R.E. shows evidence of links to Steiner and Bailey in occasional *Venture Inward* articles alluding to them. In 1996, a joint conference was held at A.R.E. headquarters co-sponsored by the Anthroposophical Society, focusing on the Steiner teachings.

Students of the Cayce readings find common ground with Steiner in a number of areas. Visionary investigations of prehistory by both seers endorse much of the Theosophical scheme of anthropogenesis found in *The Secret Doctrine*. Richard Drummond's book comparing Buddha and Christ refers to the clairvoyance of Steiner and Cayce with equal respect. Bailey, unlike Steiner, was primarily a channeler rather than an independent clairvoyant, attributing her works to "the Tibetan," Djual Kul of Theosophical literature. Unlike Steiner and Cayce, who emphasized spiritual independence and discouraged excessive interest in Masters, Bailey wrote many books in which "the Hierarchy" was the central focus. But by placing Christ as part of that hierarchy, Bailey moved away from Blavatsky's Eastern loyalties and toward the Christian esotericism represented by Steiner and Cayce. Apart from a shared Christian affiliation and a revisionist approach to Theosophy, Cayce's strongest link to Steiner and Bailey is in the area of esoteric psychology. Particularly in his integration of astrology into a holistic psychological synthesis, Cayce echoes these contemporaries more than he does Blavatsky.

As early as 1913, Rudolf Steiner was lecturing on "Man's Journey through the Planetary Spheres" and teaching that "True observation of the life between death and a new birth reveals that the forces man needs in order to repair the astral body lie in Mercury, Venus, Mars, Jupiter, Saturn, that is in the stars belonging to the planetary system."[86] Bailey's *Esoteric Astrology* is the most elaborate effort ever made to synthesize astrological tradition with Blavatskian occultism. Her emphases, however, are not very similar to those of the Cayce readings, focusing rather on a system of seven rays, which is integrated with astrology.

One question about Edgar Cayce that this book attempts to answer is "Where are the doctrines of the readings found in earlier literature?" It is a relatively simple matter to establish that Christian theosophical literature from Gnosticism to the present, esoteric psychological systems such as those of Gurdjieff, Blavatsky, and Jung, and alternative healing systems such as osteopathy, Christian Science, and naturopathy are all strongly reflected in the readings. Claims about prehistory found in nineteenth- and early twentieth-century writers such as Donnelly, Blavatsky, and Steiner are just as faithfully echoed by Cayce. But this leads to a second and far thornier question: "How did this information find its way into the readings?," to which only tentative answers are possible. The testimony of people who knew Cayce personally is unanimous in reporting that he had little conscious familiarity with the material from which his readings might, judged by their content, have borrowed. In some cases, the material closest in detail to the readings was not even published until after Cayce's death, which effectively rules out reading as a means of access to their contents.

Planetary sojourns is a theme in the readings that can only partially be traced to historical prototypes. Although soul travel among the planets of the solar system was a feature of ancient Stoicism and Gnosticism, reincarnation was not part of the equation in such systems. And among recognized sources of the reincarnation doctrine, teachings about planetary sojourns are not found until the twentieth century, and in writings that Cayce could not have read. This is particularly relevant to the question of influence from Steiner or Purucker on the astrological doctrines of the readings. Purucker's teachings on the subject were in Esoteric Section papers never published until the late 1940s, and Steiner's lectures on the subject were unavailable in English until after Cayce's death. The astrological esotericism of Max

Heindel, Alan Leo, and T. H. Burgoyne was published during Cayce's lifetime, but has less striking similarities than the other abovementioned sources noted. In the case of astrology, as with so many other aspects of the readings, the provenance of Cayce's esoteric ideas remains enigmatic.

Dreams

In thousands of readings, Cayce's interpretations cover an extremely diverse set of dreams. Most dream readings opened with a brief statement about the value of dreams. But on March 24, 1928, Cayce gave this long dissertation before proceeding to the interpretation:

> There are those that are of the purely physical nature—the reaction of properties taking in the system when digestion is not in keeping with the assimilations, and then one experiences those conditions that may be called nightmares. Then there is the mental condition of the body wherein worry, trouble, or unusual action of the mind—mentally—physically—causes seeking for the way and manner of understanding. This may bring either the action of the subconscious with the mental abilities of the body, or it may bring correlations of material sensuous conditions. These may appear in the form of visions that are in a manner then key to the situations, or they may appear in conditions as warnings, taking on conditions that are as illustrations or experiences. Then there is the action of the purely subconscious forces, giving lessons to the body out of its own experiences. These are phenomena, or experiences for a body to use, to apply, in its everyday walk of life, just as experiences of the mental condition of body may bring the better understanding of conditions to the whole body.[87]

Although Cayce provided dream readings, he always encouraged people to interpret their own dreams or spiritual experiences rather than asking others to do so, and to choose their own path of development based on the guidance received. One of the most frequently repeated admonitions in the readings echoes the Bible: "Not that ye would say as of old, who will bring down from heaven a message that we may know wisdom, or who will come from over the sea that we may hear and understand; for lo, it is in thine own heart, it is within thine own power, yea within thine own might!"[88]

Most of the categories of dreams listed by Cayce in the passage quoted are also found in *Transactions of the Blavatsky Lodge*. In response to questions from lodge members, Blavatsky divided dreams into those that are prophetic, retrospective of past lives, warnings of danger, allegorical, and those that are confused and chaotic due to physical or psychological disturbance.[89] In the most complete study of the Cayce dream interpretations to date, Harmon Bro categorizes dreams as problem solving, ESP of the past and future, and guidance for health and spiritual development.[90] The closest analogue to Cayce's approach in the psychological realm is that of Carl Jung. Like Jung, Cayce saw dreams as expressing aspects or perceptions of the unconscious mind, and advised using them as a means to greater awareness of oneself and all life. In the words of Jung, a dream is "a highly objective, natural product of the psyche, from which we might expect indications, or at least hints, about certain, basic trends in the psychic process . . . [and] to give us certain indications about the objective causality as well as about the objective tendencies . . . "[91] Sometimes, as seen in chapter 2, analyses of Cayce's own dreams are very revealing of objective issues he faced in his life. In one dream, Cayce saw the process of doing a reading as starting from a central point from which he would radiate upward in a spiral through ever-wider rings to the heavens. In another reading, this was interpreted as follows:

> As indicated, the entity is—in the affairs of the world—a tiny speck, as it were, a mere grain of sand; yet when raised in the atmosphere or realm of the spiritual forces it becomes all inclusive, as seen by the size of the funnel—which reaches not downward, nor over, but direct to that which is felt by the experience of man as into the heavens itself. As indicated in the rings, or the nets as of nerves, each portion of the sphere, or the earth, or the heavens, is in that place which has been set by an All Wise Creative Energy.[92]

This dream, then, gave a symbolic representation of the activity of Cayce's subconscious in the trance state. The greatest challenge facing any student of the readings is to explain the processes involved and the information sources accessed by the readings. The readings themselves discuss this question at considerable length, as will be discussed in the conclusion.

The Study Group Program

As of 1996, there were more than 1,500 A.R.E. study groups in existence, with possibly an equal number of non-affiliated Cayce study groups.[93] They share common features with several comparable forms of religious and psychological group work. Because the program emphasizes prayer, meditation, and healing, it corresponds to familiar organizational forms found in churches. Members are encouraged to attempt to apply the concepts discussed each week in their own lives and report their experiences to the group, which is a parallel to the Fourth Way approach as well as to traditional group psychotherapy. Since the study group readings discuss psychic experience, groups have some similarities to the "development" circles found in Spiritualism. According to Robert Wuthnow's *Christianity in the 21st Century,* one of the most widely acknowledged challenges facing the church is the creation of spiritual community.[94] His compilation *I Come Away Stronger* is devoted to reports of small groups as elements in the revival of Christianity. The intimate setting of an A.R.E. study groups can fulfill this need for community, often to a far greater degree than the churches. Averaging memberships of between eight and ten, meeting weekly, and following the same texts, the study groups form the backbone of the committed A.R.E. membership.

The texts for study groups are the two volumes entitled *A Search for God,* produced by the first study group, which was directed by a series of readings now published in their entirety as *The Study Group Readings. A Search for God, Book I* opens with a chapter on meditation, which provides a common practice for group members, usually carried out at the end of the study and discussion period. The twelve lessons are on cooperation, self-knowledge, ideals, faith, virtue and understanding, fellowship, patience, the Christ Consciousness as the "Open Door," the divine presence, the meaning of the crucifixion, the oneness of God with all manifestation, and the meaning of human and divine love. Groups normally read and discuss a few pages per week. Chairmanship of the group rotates on a weekly or per chapter basis. The first *Search for God* book was compiled by the Norfolk A.R.E. Study Group #1 over a period of eleven years, and combines excerpts from the readings with contributions by group members based on their application of the readings.

Each lesson has an affirmation given in the readings to be used with it; the first is "Not my will but Thine, O Lord, be done in and through me. Let me ever be a channel of blessings, today, now, to those that I contact in every way. Let my going in, my coming out be in accord with that Thou would have me do, and as the call comes, 'Here am I, send me, use me.' "[95] A second volume of *A Search for God* appeared five years after Cayce's death, with lessons on the themes of:

opportunity, day and night, God's manifestations in the earth, desire, destiny of the mind, destiny of the body, destiny of the soul, glory, knowledge, wisdom, happiness, and spirit. Companion volumes by Mark Thurston provide spiritual disciplines to apply the themes of each chapter, with several options per lesson. The greatest influences on the approach of these disciplines, apart from the readings themselves, seem to be Jungian psychology and "The Work" of Gurdjieff. In a more recent work, Thurston comments on Jung and Cayce as both calling the mental realm the fourth dimension, and uses a Gurdjieff parable and Fourth Way concepts.[96]

A Handbook for A.R.E. Study Groups and a booklet entitled *Edgar Cayce and Group Dynamics* guide in the formation of new groups and orient new members to the pattern that has been developed. The ideal group size is ten or fewer.[97] The handbook includes thirty-two questions for self-examination, based on Ouspensky's *The Fourth Way,* yet another sign of compatibility of approaches.[98] The goal of the groups is to promote open sharing of diverse experiences and points of view, creating an atmosphere in which the whole becomes greater than the sum of its parts. From personal observation of three study groups over a period of nearly twenty years, some general characteristics can be identified. There is rarely any unanimity of opinion in religious matters, but it is rare for different ideas about doctrine to produce interpersonal conflict in the group. Within a general atmosphere of respect and appreciation for the Cayce readings, groups include individuals with very different levels of knowledge and commitment. The shared ideal of increased understanding of oneself and others produces harmony despite great diversity. There is little emphasis on psychic abilities, medical details, or highly personal matters. The nature of the *Search for God* material draws the group focus to subjects of universal relevance for which no specialized knowledge is required. Equal participation in discussions is the norm, and group leaders are advised to encourage maximum interchange. Three crucial requirements for successful study groups were outlined in an early reading:

First, there must be the innate desire for help from the individual needing physical or spiritual assistance. Second, there must be a belief in the divine forces innate in each individual. Third, and first, there must be consciousness in the entity, or in the ones responsible for the physical and mental development of the entity, of the divine in each and every entity.[99]

The handbook lists five objectives for study groups:

1. To assist each individual to meditate and pray in an intelligent and practical manner—not only alone, but in groups.
2. To show by practical application how each one may know his relationship to God and to his fellow man.
3. To furnish a safe way for soul growth.
4. To help each member to live a balanced life.
5. To inform each member about the broad areas of information that may be found in the readings given through Edgar Cayce—information that will help to awaken him to a more spiritual and more useful life.[100]

When a group completes the *Search for God* books and their companion volumes, it may choose to return to the beginning, or use alternative material. A.R.E. provides a series of "circulating files" on a variety of topics, and these are well adapted to study group use.

Psychic Powers

Reading 294–1 has a particular importance in understanding the work of Edgar Cayce. Cayce himself was subject 294, and 1 indicates the first reading in the recorded series. Many others predated the beginning of accurate record keeping, but this reading is the first available that explains how Cayce's seemingly paranormal abilities operated:

> [Cayce's mind] has the power to interpret to the objective mind of others what it acquires from the subconscious mind of other individuals of the same kind. The subconscious mind forgets nothing. The conscious mind receives the impression from without and transfers all thought to the subconscious, where it remains even though the conscious be destroyed. The subconscious mind of Edgar Cayce is in direct communication with all other subconscious minds, and is capable of interpreting through his objective mind and imparting impressions received to other objective minds, gathering in this way all knowledge possessed by millions of other subconscious minds.[101]

The language here shows a trace of Freudian influence, but the model most consistently implied in Cayce's explanation of his own gift is that of Thomson Jay Hudson's *The Law of Psychic Phenomena*, recommended along with Ouspensky's *Tertium Organum* and James's *Variet-*

ies of Religious Experience as preparation for study group work.[102] Before Freud, Hudson had postulated that psychic phenomena were most often due to the action of the subconscious mind, which had all the abilities mentioned in the above reading. Hudson's book distinguishes between the "objective" and "subjective" mind, and Cayce used this terminology in the readings in reference to his own trance state.[103] The ordinary conscious mind is the "objective" aspect, whereas the "subjective" aspect is the seat of all the powers known to parapsychology.

Granting for the sake of argument the explanation in the readings for Cayce's clairvoyance, there remains the question of its variable accuracy. His subconscious mind may well have received and stored impressions from the subconscious minds of people receiving readings. But even if Cayce could contact "all knowledge possessed by millions" of other subconscious minds, what would filter out spurious "knowledge"? According to this model, all the falsehoods believed in by any subconscious mind are part of the storehouse which is accessed clairvoyantly. Thus, a judging function is necessary to evaluate the perceptions conveyed by the subconscious. Yet Cayce consistently denied the ability to judge and evaluate what came through him. Harmon Bro emphasizes the dominance of intuition in his appraisal of Cayce according to Jungian personality types.[104] He was as perplexed as anyone else when details about reincarnation, Atlantis, and the Great White Brotherhood began to emerge in the readings. His biographers are unanimous in agreeing that Cayce lacked much familiarity with book-learning in the fields he discussed in trance. He himself wrote (in a conscious state) "I've read very little of the philosophers of the ages."[105] Harmon Bro notes in *A Seer Out of Season* that the bookshelves in Cayce's office were nearly bare, and his wife Gertrude's collection of the novels of E. P. Roe dominated the shelves in their living quarters.[106] Yet the ability to instantly grasp the contents of a book seems to have persisted beyond his childhood spelling tests, since he also wrote, "A few days ago I was talking to some people and they told me about a book that had been written by some of the masters from the Far East. I had never seen the book before, but when I opened it to read it, I knew what was in it before I read it. I don't know how, or why—but I knew the experiences I was going to encounter."[107] Gina Cerminara reports that Cayce often received gift books on esoteric subjects from admirers but never read them, preferring to spend his spare time fishing and gardening.[108] Thomas Sugrue observed that neither Edgar nor Gertrude read metaphysical or scholarly books, and that their library was mainly popular fiction.[109] Nevertheless, one of Cayce's skeptical critics, Martin Gardner, assumes without any evidence that he was a voracious reader of books from which he might have derived the contents of his readings.[110] Unless there was a massive conspiracy to conceal and deny Cayce's actual literary interests, his primary access to the information in the readings was not through books. Charles Thomas Cayce suggested that conversation and correspondence are more fruitful avenues of approach than books, if one is seeking "normal" explanations for the information in the readings. Yet there remains a substratum of material that does not yield to normal explanations. This includes both the evidences of distant viewing discussed in chapter 1 and the doctrinal elements in which the readings parallel sources that Cayce did not know. The implication of this chapter is that the readings' psychology seems like a skillful blend of Blavatsky, Gurdjieff, and Jung, along with some idiosyncratic elements. Examination of the readings on CD-ROM, however, supports the hypothesis that Cayce was not consciously familiar with any of these authors. In the case of Blavatsky, most of the fourteen mentions of her name in the CD-ROM were made in letters from people who sought readings; the handful of references in the readings themselves and in Cayce's letters were in response to specific questions and indicate no familiarity with her works. Gurdjieff and Ouspensky are even less frequently cited, and Jung's name appears only eight times, never in a reading. In all these cases, there is evidence that persons seeking readings were familiar with the various psychological systems, but no evidence that Cayce himself was at all knowledgeable of any of them. Although the readings refer to the "akashic records" as sources, they also make it clear that these records are found within the individual, "written upon the skein of time and space by the activity of the mental self."[111]

There were a number of instances in which Cayce's clairvoyance failed quite obviously. Sometimes he simply slept, and never responded to hypnotic suggestions. Occasionally subjects of readings complained that they saw no value or relevance at all in the material, in which case their fees were immediately returned. On two occasions, a medical reading was given for someone who had died that day, and discussed the patient as if still living. (At other times Cayce was definite about the death of the subject, which was subsequently confirmed.) Such circumstances caused those in his circle to ask for explanations of the ways the readings could fail to produce accurate information. Among possible reasons for failure, the reading listed poor health or psychological resistance in Cayce and "the mental attitude of those about the body that are not in accord with the type, class and character of information sought . . . "[112] This included the people in Cayce's presence at the time of the reading as well as the subject, who might be hundreds of miles away but was expected to maintain a prayerful state at the time the reading was given.

Rarely, in less than one percent of the readings, Cayce performed traditional mediumship in which discarnate or angelic spirits spoke through him.[113] The readings take a dim view of Spiritualism, however, often implying that it is to be avoided. They say that "No greater psychic lived than Jesus of Nazareth,"[114] and advise persons wishing to discern the quality of communicating spirits to "ask that they acknowledge the life, the death, the resurrection of the Jesus, the Christ."[115] Possession is described as a genuine danger, and practices like automatic writing and ouija boards are discouraged. A balanced approach was strongly recommended; the readings distinguish between the mystic, the psychic, and the occult, saying that although they are one, "mystic is as the spirit or the activity, whereas the psychic is the soul, the occult is the mind. Do not confuse; for each in their respective sphere—if and when taken alone—becomes confusing."[116] As this passage indicates, psychic experience was always regarded as of lesser importance than spiritual awakening and mental comprehension. To the present, the A.R.E. emphasizes the need for balance among these different levels of being; the study group materials are particularly insistent on this issue.

There was only one so-called psychic power that Cayce practiced publicly in his conscious personality. He had a consistent ability to see and read auras. Thomas Sugrue comments that "because it functioned while he was fully conscious," the ability "intrigued him more than his gift for giving readings."[117] The small booklet on auras published by A.R.E. is the most substantial of Cayce's conscious literary works, otherwise limited to articles of a few pages. Even this nineteen-page booklet was possible only through Sugrue's collaboration. In his introduction, he comments that when asked to write such a booklet, Cayce "gave his usual answer—that he didn't know enough about the subject, had no background in it, etc., ad infinitum. He had a very low opinion of anything he said while awake."[118] In the booklet, Cayce says that he would never think of reading auras professionally, and was better able to read them for people he knew than for strangers. But he predicted that the time would come when this ability would be universal, and he wanted to promote its acceptance. In a color chart at the end of the booklet, these correspondences are given: red—force, vigor, energy, nervousness, egotism; orange—thoughtfulness, consideration, laziness, repression; yellow—health, well-being, friendliness, timidity, weakness of will; green—healing, helpful, but deceit when mixed with yellow; blue—spiritual, artistic, selfless, struggle, melancholy; indigo and violet—seeking, religions, heart & stomach trouble.[119]

Meditation

Meditation appears first in the list of study group objectives; its priority in the A.R.E. is further indicated by the fact that two of the first three volumes in the Edgar Cayce Library Series are entirely devoted to the subject. Cayce's basic instructions are simple and clear, and are summarized in a reading:

> Cleanse the body with pure water. Sit or lie in an easy position. Breathe in through the right nostril three times, and exhale through the mouth. Breathe in three times through the left nostril and out through the right. Then, either with the aid of a low music, or the incantating of that which carries self deeper— deeper—to the seeing, feeling, experiencing of that image in the creative forces of love, enter into the Holy of Holies. As self feels or experiencing the raising of this, see it disseminated through the *inner* eye (not the carnal eye) to that which will bring the greater understanding in meeting every condition in the experience of the body. Then listen to the music that is made as each center of thine own body responds to that new creative force that is being, and that *is* disseminated through its own channel; and we will find that little by little this entering in will enable self to renew all that is necessary—in Him.[120]

This passage is strikingly similar to the meditation instructions of surat shabd yoga as taught by the Radhasoami sects of Hinduism. In another reading, Cayce states that the divine presence is found "in thine own tabernacle," in the holy of holies, in the third eye—*not* above same!"[121] The third eye is identical to what Radhasoami calls the eye center. Surat shabd yoga is designed to enable the individual spark of divinity (surat) to attain union (yoga) with its source through the audible sound current (shabd) or voice of the silence. The first step in attaining this is called simran, and involves repetition of divine names while concentrating attention at the point just above and between the eyes. This is "the portal from which it can flee the physical form."[122] Having succeeded in this concentration, one is then ready for the practice of bhajan or song, defined as "several melodies, one for each region of consciousness," which guide the soul towards its divine source.[123] The first sound that is to be followed into the astral plane is that of a "deeply resonant bell"; as one hears the subsequent melodies, distinctive lights are seen in each region.[124]

Cayce refers to both lights and sounds that are experienced as a result of concentrating attention at the third eye. Concerning the sound, he advised that one meditate on one's highest ideal, and then:

> [R]aise the vibrations from thy lower self, thy lower conscious-
> ness through the centers of thy body to the temple of thy mind,
> thy brain, thy eye that is single in purpose, or to the glandular
> forces of the body as the Single Eye. Then, listen—listen! For it
> is not in the storm, not in the noise, but in the still small voice
> that rises within![125]

Study Group readings include answers to questions about auditory, visual, tactile, and emotional experiences during meditation. Another parallel to Radhasoami practice is found in one of these questions. Radhasoami gurus teach that the sound to be followed in meditation is heard on the right side of the head. When asked about a roaring sound in the right ear heard in meditation, Cayce replied:

> Thou has heard that the Voice of Him cometh as the rushing of
> mighty waters; and that injunction which came with same,
> *"Peace—be still."* For it is not only in the storm, nor the rocks, but
> rather the still small voice that comes after same. Hence thou
> hast drawn, and do draw, nigh unto the brink of a greater under-
> standing.[126]

Questions about lights seen during meditation practice were also common. Cayce, unlike Radhasoami gurus, taught that the white light was the highest and should be followed, for "More and more as the white light comes to thee, more and more will there be the awakening . . . the light of the throne of mercy itself."[127]

Another striking parallel between Cayce and Radhasoami on meditation is the recommended time for its practice. According to the readings, the best time for meditation is "two to three o'clock in the morning."[128] Radhasoami teaches the need for a longer period of meditation, two and one half hours, but advises beginning at 2:00 or 3:00 A.M. according to different texts. Since no Radhasoami literature was widely available in the United States until 1934 (Julian Johnson's *With a Great Master in India* being the first), after Cayce had already given his meditation guidelines, literary influence is not a very plausible basis for the similarities. But long before Cayce, a Westerner wrote a book advising Radhasoami techniques without referring to that religion as their source. In 1889, H. P. Blavatsky published *The Voice of the Silence*, purportedly a translation of fragments from something called *The Book of the Golden Precepts*, which she had memorized in her studies many years before. It advises the meditator to:

> [L]et the fiery power retire into the inmost chamber, the chamber of the Heart, and the abode of the World's Mother. Then from the heart that Power shall rise into the sixth, the middle region, the place between thine eyes, when it becomes the breath of the ONE-SOUL, the voice which filleth all, thy Master's voice . . . thou hast to hear the voice of the *inner* GOD in seven manners . . [129]

In this passage, Blavatsky identifies the voice of the Master with the sound heard as a result of concentrating one's energy at the Third Eye. But apart from this passage, there is no instruction in Blavatsky's writings concerning this technique. Radhasoami is even more oriented to Masters than is Theosophy; the disciple can only be initiated by a legitimate Master, and after initiation he or she is allegedly aided by this initiating Master in the inner planes during meditation. The Bible of Radhasoami, *Sar Bachan*, by the movement's founder Shiv Dayal Singh, states that "You cannot see the Lord anywhere except within yourself, or within a perfect Sadh or Saint . . . "[130] Despite their insistence on the one Master of Masters, the Christ Consciousness, the Cayce readings echo Radhasoami and Theosophy in stating that "We have a body, one capable of attuning even to the masters of the holy place, or holy mount."[131] Nevertheless, another passage suggests that the higher self is the main objective of practices involving hearing the divine sound: "there is a *definite* connection between that we have chosen to term the sixth sense, or acting through the auditory forces of the body-physical, and the other self within self."[132]

There are clear-cut differences in approach between the readings and the Radhasoami teachings, with attendant differences of technique. Radhasoami defines the Third Eye as the highest of six centers; the *Sar Bachan* states "The first ganglion is just behind the eyes and is the abode of the Surat or Rooh (Soul). From this center it spreads by degrees into the body, through the five lower centers."[133] The readings, on the other hand, regard the Third Eye as the second of seven centers, and as the place where energy from the lower centers is transformed and recirculated. Cayce refers to the "kundaline forces as they act along the spine," aroused by the "opening of the centers of the body."[134] While Radhasoami initiates are taught to work directly with the Third Eye rather than to raise kundalini, their goal of meeting God through this practice is similar to that of Cayce's meditation technique. Although advising the meditator to regard the process as enabling one to receive "the Lord, thy God," who has "promised to meet thee there," he makes it clear that it is the work of a lifetime to manifest the results: "And there *shall* it be told thee from within the steps thou shouldst take day by day, step by step. Not that some great exploit, some great manner of change should come within thine body, thine mind, but line upon line, precept upon precept, here a little, there a little. For it is, as He has given, not the knowledge alone but the practical application—in thine daily experience with thy fellow man—that counts."[135]

Radhasoami is not the only source of parallels to Cayce's meditation instructions. David Bell points out that Baird T. Spaldings's series *Life and Teaching of the Masters of the Far East* contains "many of Cayce's most important ideas—such as the role of ideals in three-dimensional consciousness, or the connection between the chakras and the seven ductless glands,"[136] but also that Cayce described the author as "not authentic."[137] The Theosophist Charles W. Leadbeater helped introduce chakras and kundalini to a popular Western audience and interpreted *Revelation* as symbolic of the kundalini experience before Cayce did so.[138] Leadbeater is briefly quoted in one reading, but not in any context that suggests he influenced Cayce's ideas on meditation or clairvoyance.[139] The very idea of a life reading, however, seemingly introduced by Lammers, a student of Theosophy, might owe something to Leadbeater's *Lives of Alcyone.*

The Christian keynote of meditation as taught in the readings is found in Cayce's interpretation of the Lord's Prayer. The individual is advised to apply the prayer as an esoteric guide to meditation in which each phrase evokes a different stage in the movement of energy through the body's spiritual centers, which are linked with endocrine glands. Opening with, "Our father, who art in heaven," the meditator feels the spiritual energy drawn into the pituitary gland (crown chakra). Saying, "Hallowed be thy name," one is to feel the energy come down to the pineal gland (brow chakra). "Thy kingdom come, thy will be done" is said as the energy is drawn to the thyroid gland (throat chakra). "On earth as it is in heaven" completes the descending phase of the meditation, as the energy comes to the thymus gland (heart chakra). The psychological meaning of this drawing down of energy from the crown to the heart is an acknowledgment of one's rootedness in the divine. Invoking the heavenly father is a means of awakening one's own higher self; reference to the Hallowed name alludes to the power of divine names as a way of making contact with the spiritual realms. ("Nam," which means "name," is one of the primary mantras used in simran meditation at the eye center in Radhasoami.) After hallowing the name is the coming of the kingdom and the doing of the will, which requires the descent of spiritual energy into the mental body. Bringing spiritual and mental energies into physical-plane expression, "on earth as in heaven," is symbolized by the use of the heart chakra as a receptacle. The second, ascending portion of the prayer starts with the phrase "Give us this day our daily bread," associated by Cayce with the gonads (root chakra). The gonads are said to be connected to a gland called the Lyden, the "closed gland" and keeper "of the door, that would loose and let either passion or the miracle to be loosed to enable those seeking to find the Open Door, or the Way to find expression in the attributes of the imaginative forces of a body... "[140] "Lead us not into temptation" draws the energy through this lyden gland, and "Forgive us our debts, as we forgive our debtors" is said while feeling the energy at the adrenals (navel chakra). As noted in chapter 1, there is no lyden gland known to anatomy. A.R.E. books equate it with the cells of Leydig, interstitial cells in the testicles that produce testosterone, and their ovarian counterparts. As the meditator prays, "But deliver us from evil," the energy is brought back to the thymus and heart chakra. The need for forgiveness can be plausibly associated with the adrenals, source of adrenaline, the "fight or flight" hormone that stimulates aggression. The association between the heart and deliverance from evil seems to imply a request for purification of the emotions. The prayer concludes with, "For thine is the kingdom," at which the energy rises to the thyroid gland/throat chakra, "and the Power," as it rises to the pineal gland/ brow chakra, and finally "And the Glory. Forever," at which point the energy returns to the pituitary/crown. Once the circuit has been completed, the prayer phase is followed by a silent meditation in which the energies raised at the outset are distributed within the body and spiritual centers. These are also associated with the seven churches of Revelation.[141] The readings identify Jupiter with the pituitary, Mercury with the pineal, Uranus with the thyroid, Venus with the thymus, Mars with the adrenals, Neptune with the Lyden/Leydig, and Saturn with the gonads.[142] Both the pineal and Leydig are the "seat of the soul,"[143] called the open and closed doors respectively.

In his sevenfold enumeration of the spiritual centers, Cayce echoes the esoteric systems of Blavatsky and Gurdjieff, although with somewhat different emphases. Blavatsky taught her inner group that "the Pineal corresponds with Divine Thought."[144] She named the seven centers as "between the eyebrows," "spleen and liver," "stomach," "the region of the umbilical cord," "heart," "pineal gland," and "the akasa that fills the skull."[145] Although this seems to avoid any centers below the waist, elsewhere she taught the group that "the pineal gland, at the upper pole of the human body, corresponds with the Uterus (in the female and its analogue in the male) at the lower pole," adding that "the Pituitary body is only the servant of the pineal gland, its torch-bearer."[146]

According to the Cayce readings, seven is the number of "spiritual forces that are activative."[147] This parallels Theosophy's doctrine of seven human principles, degrees of initiation, and phases of cosmic cycles (i.e., rounds and races). Gurdjieff classifies seven stages of individual development and seven subtle centers. The closest analogue in earlier esotericism to such sevenfold systems is found not in Hinduism but in Islam. In the system of Alaoddawleh Semnani, there are seven suprasensory organs or *latifa*. Semnani, an Iranian Sufi of the thirteenth–fourteenth centuries, built his system on the metaphysics of Suhrawardi, based on light and optics. Stages of spiritual illumination correspond to different colored lights. The heart, rather than the pineal, is the primary physical focus for spiritual consciousness in his and other Sufi systems. Henri Corbin writes, "The mystic is aware of this growth thanks to the apperception of colored lights which characterize each of the suprasensory organs or centers,"[148] but their sequence given by Semnani has little in common with Cayce's or earlier Sufi sequences. Although Semnani sees the penultimate stage as contact with "the Jesus of your being," he places beyond this a final stage of the "Muhammad of your being."[149] Semnani defines black and green lights as the highest stages; Cayce associates green with healing, blue with trust, and purple with strength; but when the meditator sees white light, it is "the light of the throne of mercy itself."[150]

The goal of meditation, according to the readings, is "becoming conscious of the God-force, which is a part of the consciousness" and "application of a spiritual truth through the mental process to produce the fruits of the spirit in your own physical consciousness."[151] The central purpose or ideal in presenting the work of the A.R.E. is that "The Truth that shall make you free in body, in mind, and one *with* the living force that may express itself in individual lives . . . "[152] Cayce's meditation guidelines oppose those of Radhasoami in their valuation of earthly embodiment. When one reaches the Third Eye in Radhasoami meditation, this is used as a portal through which one can leave the body. Through surat shabd yoga the meditator is eventually to gain liberation from rebirth, which is the highest good. Physical and mental well-being are regarded as irrelevant to such a high pursuit. With Cayce, on the other hand, the Third Eye is the meeting place of the mind, body, and spirit, to be used for their integration and balance. Benefits to the physical and mental health of the practitioner are regarded as a crucial reason for meditation, and the goal of escaping rebirth is never promoted. Nevertheless, the readings balance their emphasis on physical health and mental/emotional well-being with an insistence that our true home is not earthly. Meditation is to remind us of our proper focus, the source from which all proceeds and to which all must return: "Keep the body, the mind, the soul, in attune with the spheres of celestial forces, rather than of earthly forces. Rather than listening to that which is poetically given as to the voice that arises from the earth, listen to that which comes as the music of the spheres . . . "[153]

The Guru Connection

Links between the A.R.E. and the Radhasoami tradition developed during the lifetime of Edgar Cayce and continued under the leadership of Hugh Lynn. Bhagat Singh Thind is the most likely influence behind Radhasoami elements in the readings. Thind, a Sikh from Amritsar, India, first gained fame in a 1923 court case against the United States in which he sought to overturn restrictions on immigration by East Indians on the grounds that they were Caucasian.[154] The lawsuit failed and Thind returned to Amritsar where he began to write books expounding his Westernized form of Sikhism. His early books bore little resemblance to Radhasoami teaching, but by the early 1930s he had returned to America after being initiated by Sawan Singh of Radhasoami Satsang—Beas.[155] Henceforth he referred to himself only as a Sikh, and denied any connection to Sawan Singh. According to David C. Lane, Thind taught classes throughout the country.[156] Lane's interview with Mrs. Thind in 1977 elicited her claim that Thind's initiator was a guru in the Himalayas and a denial of his association with Radhasoami.[157] Andrea Diem, author of a dissertation on shabd yoga groups in North America, comments that claims of mysterious Himalayan initiations are "a story that appears to be common among those who wish to deny any certifiable historical link."[158] Unlike traditional Radhasoami gurus, Thind charged for his services in the "Sikh Study Groups" to which he attracted several hundred disciples.[159]

Thind self-published several books, most presenting Radhasoami doctrines without acknowledging them as such. His early work *The House of Happiness* (1930) is not particularly Radhasoami oriented, and bears some signs of Theosophical influence. Although written before his acquaintance with Cayce, it agrees with some of contents of the readings. Thind refers to "the Masters of Wisdom" in Theosophical terms, as a group of beings "higher than ourselves, [who] have conquered death and dedicated themselves to the service of humanity... "[160] Jesus is identified with these Masters, who are alleged to have taken him to India as a child and taught him in "all the occult sciences"; he then went to Persia before returning home.[161] Thind refers to Ouspensky's *Tertium Organum* and teaches that "mind and higher spiritual planes are all seven-fold."[162] He claims that "Aum is the most sacred word of the Scriptures,"[163] agreeing with Blavatsky rather than the Radhasoami gurus. Thind instructed meditators to chant Aum seated upright with an erect spine, while fixing attention on the crown or brow chakra.[164] This suggests some familiarity with Radhasoami techniques, but it was not until 1939 that he published *The Radiant Road to Reality*, in which he clearly emerges in the surat shabd yoga tradition. This book includes extensive plagiarisms of Julian Johnson's *With a Great Master in India.* Johnson, chief Western propagandist for the Radhasoami Satsang—Beas, was later plagiarized to a far greater extent by Paul Twitchell, founder of Eckankar. Interestingly, Johnson and Twitchell were both Kentuckians like Cayce. *The Radiant Road to Reality* also includes two pages lifted from Blavatsky's *The Voice of the Silence.* Her words are placed in quotes but no source is given. Another book, published in 1957, *The Science of Union with God Here and Now,* indicates his interest in reconciling Christianity with Indian religion: "The bridge between the outer and the inner, the unifying power is the Word of God, the Holy Shabad. The true name is the involved word, the Christos. In the silence is found the word ... the living presence within the being of man, when listened to with astral ears, it regenerates the man, gives his soul the bath of bliss, and washes away all its stains and renders it immaculate."[165]

Thind's modifications to Radhasoami doctrine were few. He did not impose strict requirements for initiation, unlike Radhasoami gurus who insisted on vegetarianism, abstinence from alcohol and drugs, and two and a half hours of daily meditation.[166] Apart from charging money for his services, Thind's teachings were nearly identical to those of the Beas group, and Diem notes that some of Thind's disciples became prominent leaders in Beas and related groups after his death.[167]

Bhagat Singh Thind's only reading from Cayce was given at the home of David Kahn in New York on March 23, 1935. He was told that his most recent lifetime had been as an English immigrant to America named Bainbridge; this also describes Cayce's alleged last lifetime,

which suggests a family relationship. Before that, Thind was said to
have been a Muslim in Poona, India, and to have had several other
lifetimes in India and adjacent lands. The reading said he could reach
the age of 150; in fact he died in his mid-seventies. His final question
was "What can I contribute to the freedom of India and the brotherhood of man?" Cayce answered:

> This is a tall order, my brother!
>   The brotherhood of man—preach it ever! O, that man would
> gain the understanding in his heart of this universality of the
> truth, that man IS his brother's keeper! Then may there be the
> awakening within each soul of the necessity of its giving expres-
> sion to those in every walk of life.
>   As to the uplift of India, that in which it has been and is so
> oft misunderstood, the entity's greater contribution may be to
> the world as to the truths that India holds and has held that the
> world so much needs, in its mad rush for the expression of the
> desires of the flesh.[168]

Gladys Davis noted at the time:

> After the above reading Dr. Thind talked about himself and how
> beautifully the Life Reading fit him. He had studied philoso-
> phies and religions of the world. After reading Emerson, Whitman
> and Thoreau he became inspired to travel to America to fulfill
> his destiny as a Spiritual Teacher. He arrived here just before his
> twentieth birthday. He was one of the very few East Indians in
> the United States during World War One.[169]

The next day, March 24, Davis wrote to an inquirer that "Dr. Thind's
lectures will help you to understand the importance and necessity of
positive constructive thinking."[170] On March 31, another woman was
told in a reading that she had been a disciple of Thind in a past life,
when his name was Saneid.[171] She later asked how to be of help to
Thind in her physical culture work, which suggests that she was his
disciple in her present life.

In June 1935, Thind attended the Fourth Annual Congress of the
A.R.E. in Virginia Beach, where he gave Cayce a photograph of himself, inscribed "To My beloved friend and brother, Mr. Edgar Cayce,
with my sincerest blessing and love. Radiantly yours, Dr. Thind."[172]
Cayce hung this in the room where he gave readings, which was
adorned with pictures of many of his supporters. Thind gave a pre-

sentation at the Congress, and two weeks later wrote to Cayce expressing his "genuine and heartfelt thanks for the courtesy, consideration and comradeship that I enjoyed while with you and yours. I can never forget the good people who love you so dearly and who came to see and hear me, while in Norfolk!"[173]

On April 4, 1936, Thind wrote a letter to Cayce offering free use of his hall in New York for whatever purposes Cayce might require.[174] Thind's organization bore the name Institute of Applied Truth and met at 200 West 57th St.[175] A few months later, Cayce gave approval for the use of Thind's breathing exercises in a reading for a woman in New York.[176] In a letter dated September 19, 1936, Cayce referred to Thind as one of four "research investigators" who had analyzed the life readings and commented on their constructive nature.[177] In 1940, Gladys Davis noted that she had been told Thind had married an American woman (according to Lane, who met her, this was incorrect) and was continuing to lecture and give classes.[178] Hugh Lynn Cayce "attended Dr. Thind's meditation class again, while lecturing in the same city" in 1953.[179] The final entry in Davis's reports on Thind is dated September 15, 1967:

> He died suddenly without warning, for he apparently was in excellent health. His wife and a son and daughter survived him, and two grandchildren. In 52 years of lecturing he spoke to at least 5 million Americans, teaching them to become companionate with their own indwelling Father. Thousands were initiated as disciples into the Inner Life, and the discovery of the power of the Holy Nam. He was also the author of many illuminating books, the last three of which dealt with Jesus, the Christ: "They serve as a springboard to greater spiritual heights, wherein one appreciates more than ever the message of the Sat Gurus, the Saviours, Avatars, the Christs, of which Jesus the Christ was one."
>
> He never forgot his debt to his motherland. India was under British rule at the time he arrived in America at the age of twenty. In the years to follow he made outstanding sacrifices as a pioneer in India's Independence movement, and in helping East Indians gain their citizenship in this country—denied until 1946. Many Indian students in America completed their education with his financial assistance. Some returned to India and became members of Parliament, Chief Ministers, doctors, and scientists.[180]

A future guru in the Radhasoami tradition was active in the A.R.E. during the years after Thind's death. Ishwar Chandra Sharma,

Ph.D. taught in Tidewater area colleges and universities in the 1960s
and '70s, and frequently visited the A.R.E. headquarters from 1969
through 1971 pursuing research on the readings. A. Robert Smith's
biography of Hugh Lynn reports that a 1970 lecture by Sharma of-
fended the A.R.E. President so deeply that he walked out of the room
after telling Sharma, "You don't know what you are talking about."[181]
(This was occasioned by Sharma's speculation that Jesus did not suffer
on the cross due to yogic techniques he learned in India.) In 1975, Sharma,
then chairman of the philosophy department at the University of
Udaipur, wrote a book entitled *Cayce, Karma and Reincarnation,* published by Theosophical Publishing House in Wheaton, Illinois. At the
time he was also visiting professor of philosophy at Christopher Newport College in Newport News, Virginia. There was presumably no
permanent alienation between Sharma and the A.R.E., for in his introduction to the book, Hugh Lynn Cayce called him the first "highly
trained, scholarly, Eastern philosopher" to write a study of the Cayce
readings, a study that built "some bridges between Eastern and Western
philosophy, using Edgar Cayce's concepts as planks in the bridge."[182]
This is a fair summary of the book, which specifically reconciles Hinduism with Christianity by means of the readings. Andrea Diem calls
Sharma "the first bona fide American Radhasoami guru," since he spent
more than ten years in the United States and succeeded his own guru,
Faqir Chand, upon the latter's death in 1981. Faqir Chand was the
successor of Shiv Brat Lal, who had toured the United States and other
countries in 1911 spreading the Radhasoami message.[183] It was probably
through Sharma's agency that Hugh Lynn and a group of A.R.E. leaders
visited Faqir Chand on a tour of India in 1968. David C. Lane, who
interviewed Faqir Chand on several occasions in the 1970s, recalls that
the guru "was sponsored by A.R.E. during one of his trips; he also had
a nice letter from A.R.E. on the wall of his ashram and he showed it to
me with great fondness. He mentioned Cayce to me and he also said
that several in A.R.E. took him to be a guru."[184]

    The implications of Cayce's acquaintance with Bhagat Singh Thind
are not immediately obvious. On one hand, there is evidence here as
in many other cases showing that Cayce was acquainted with people
familiar with teachings that find parallels in the readings. Nowhere is
there a major element in the readings that does not appear elsewhere
in published literature, although emphases and details are often unique,
and the overall synthesis is clearly Cayce's own. More to the point,
one can always find links whereby Cayce might have learned of these
doctrines through his acquaintances. On the other hand, chronology
does not support a straightforward case of influence (much less bor-

rowing or plagiarism). The readings' basic outline of meditation appeared in 1932, three years before Thind appeared on the A.R.E. scene. One might speculate that some of Thind's disciples were among Cayce's acquaintances by that time, but no evidence has been found to confirm such an influence.

This leads to the more general question of influence, borrowing, or plagiarism in the readings. As a librarian, I have approached the readings as a bibliographic mystery. One of the foremost questions involved in my research was, "In what books could Cayce have found the doctrines that are presented in the readings?" But having answered this to a certain extent (albeit less than in David Bell's lengthy and exhaustive study), I find a mystery confounding the effort to explain how such material made its way into the readings. The two most extreme possible explanations will only ring true to partisans of extremist perspectives. On the true believer end of the spectrum, this would be to say that Cayce accessed a body of objective truth in the Akashic records, and any similarities to published works available in his time would be coincidental, or due to the other authors' access to the same records. Only slightly less dogmatic would be the assertion that all this material is in the Collective Unconscious, where Cayce and the authors he parallels obtained it. At the other end of the spectrum would be the extremist skeptic, who would insist that Cayce had read all the parallel material necessary to concoct the readings, and concealed having done so. The problem with such an argument is that every eyewitness denies it, including people who spent years of their lives around Cayce. Either he concealed his voluminous reading from all his family and friends, or they too were part of a conspiracy to conceal the bibliographic sources of the readings. In addition to all the eyewitness testimonies to Cayce's lack of literary familiarity with esotericism and other parallel doctrines, the inquirer has tens of thousands of pages of his correspondence to consider as evidence. Occasionally, Cayce admits to reading a work with obvious parallels in the readings, for example *A Dweller on Two Planets*.[185] But again and again, in the cases of Blavatsky, Steiner, Freud, Ouspensky, and others, the correspondence reveals that it is the recipients of the readings who are familiar with the literature in question, while Cayce is not. The Bible is consistently the sole source with which he shows deep familiarity. Even when Cayce shows some familiarity with a book, it is almost always in response to an inquirer who is obviously much more fully acquainted with the source.

Indeed, for virtually every literary source that is parallel to the readings, one can find a readings recipient who is familiar with that source and has mentioned it to Cayce. The bibliography of works from which one might have concocted the system of teachings in the readings is primarily a list of books read by Cayce's counselees and not by the seer himself.

How, then, to explain the means whereby ideas digested by readings recipients found their way into readings given by a man far less familiar with the ideas? Occam's razor requires that one seek the simplest explanation first. In this case, conversation and correspondence may account for a large share of the transmission of ideas from counselees to Cayce. But it should be remembered that the correspondence rarely involved the counselees expounding at length on the doctrines that interested them; usually, they simply asked questions that referred to such matters. Conversation would thus be a more fruitful source whereby Cayce might have digested such material.

One element that should not be overlooked is that the readings occurred in a trance state. Without resorting to paranormal explanations, one should note that trance provides for a heightened suggestibility and empathy that can partly explain Cayce's uncanny ability to "get inside the heads" of his counselees. The foremost figure in the use of trance in psychotherapy was Milton Erickson (d1980), who has inspired a school of Ericksonian therapy. The Fifth International Congress on Erickson Approaches to Hypnosis and Psychotherapy focused on his methods, which included trance states for the therapist as well as the client. Sidney Rosen, a presenter at the Congress, explains "the nature of a hypnotic trance" as it affects a therapeutic encounter:

[A] trance is not a state of being asleep, unconscious, or "under." . . . Trance is a state of hypersuggestibility. . . . If the suggestions are designed to focus attention, it will then tend to be focused on a designated object or mode of experiencing or thinking. And, of course, in a trance one can be more in touch than usual with what we call the Unconscious Mind. In fact, Erickson's last definition of hypnosis was that hypnosis is the evocation and utilization of unconscious learnings.

Hypnosis can make possible intense communication between people, communication on more levels than usual. Many have had the experience, when in a trance while working therapeutically, of responding to our patient's mood and thoughts even before they were verbalized. It seemed like mind reading, but undoubtedly it came from increased sensitivity and increased recollection of past patterns of thinking, as well as an increased awareness of minimal sensory and bodily clues.[186]

In a sense, for life readings Cayce was entering trance for psychotherapeutic purposes, and therefore Rosen's observations are valuable as testimony from someone with firsthand experience of the process. But Cayce's trances were profound, and he appeared to be completely "under" and unconscious of his surroundings, unlike the therapeutic trances of Ericksonian practice. Rosen summarily dismisses "mind-reading" and attributes the uncanny aspects of trance communication with clients to normal factors. Without accepting his sweeping dismissal of telepathy, one can still admit that the normal elements he reports might have contributed to Cayce's readings. The suggestions Cayce was given were designed to focus attention on a specific object (the counselee) and a mode of experiencing or thinking (life or medical readings). In a trance state, he had expanded access to "unconscious learnings" as well as to whatever clues may have been provided by the client. But does this suffice to explain what occurred in Cayce's readings?

The best evidence, in quality as well as quantity, for a paranormal element in Cayce's work is found in the medical readings. The life, work, dream, and Study Group readings all lend themselves to reductionist analysis that would minimize the need for paranormal explanations. One can usually find normal means whereby the material therein might have been acquired by Cayce. But the kind of specific, detailed medical information provided about strangers whom Cayce never met remains the strongest evidence for his genuine clairvoyance and telepathy. Since he appears to have displayed psi ability in the medical readings, which constitute two-thirds of his work, one cannot dismiss the possibility that the life readings also contain elements of extrasensory perception. Whatever role that may have played, however, was in interaction with a plethora of normal factors: Cayce's knowledge conscious and unconscious, his communications with the client, and the nature of hypnotic suggestion itself.

Unlike Bhagat Singh Thind or Paul Twitchell, Cayce did not consciously borrow from any of the apparent sources of influence in the readings. Somewhat more relevant is the case of Ellen G. White, who propounded a similarly eclectic mix of alternative therapies in a career that overlapped Cayce's. She was subject to trance visions, and produced voluminous writings on health and religious subjects. Her biographer Ronald Numbers notes that "In her anxiety to appear uninfluenced by any earthly agency . . . Ellen White failed to mention certain pertinent facts."[187] He points out that "Even during her lifetime, people noticed hundreds of parallel passages in her writings and those of other authors, including L. B. Coles's *Philosophy of Health*."[188]

After her death, far more evidence of borrowing was discovered. White, like Thind, Twitchell, and others who built new religious teachings on borrowed material, exemplifies a pattern identified by Lane as "genealogical dissociation." This is the denial and suppression of actual sources of one's ideas in order to claim direct inspiration from a higher source. If Cayce exemplifies genealogical dissociation, it is in a drastically different way from these other examples. He did not set out to create a new religion, and was motivated primarily by the wish to be of service to individuals. He did not read most of the writings that were in some sense source materials for the ideas in the readings. And he left behind an impressive body of evidence that allows for the possibility of genuine extrasensory perception.

Richard Broughton, Director of Research at the Institute for Parapsychology in Durham, North Carolina, comments in his *Parapsychology: The Controversial Science* that no breakthrough in understanding ESP appears imminent. "At best we can hope for a gradual increase in our understanding of the mind's mysteries, born of patient and meticulous experimentation."[189] An "enormous amount of evidence for what we call psychic ability" has yet to be explained.[190] Some paradigms of materialist science define psi phenomena as impossible, but this is far from settled among physicists. Even accounting for fraud, malobservation, etc., "hundreds and hundreds of experiments in parapsychology have provided good evidence of psi phenomena,"[191] and those who dismiss decades of such findings appear motivated by dogmas rather than sincere questioning. But we are still far from having the knowledge necessary to understand Cayce.

Edgar Cayce evokes superlatives in a surprising number of different domains. His Christian theosophy is the most influential restatement of theosophical ideas in this century, at least in the English-speaking world. Moreover, the New Age movement probably owes as much to Cayce as to any other single person. He has generated more books, more widely read, than any American in the history of new religious movements of this century. As is often repeated, Cayce is the best documented psychic seer in history and the greatest impact of his work has probably been on the holistic health movement. But in appraising the significance of the four aspects of his career described in these pages, one is obliged to recognize his esoteric psychology as crucially important. As Harmon Bro notes in his dissertation, "But since his moral and religious teaching were not essentially new in the history of religions, although new on the American scene in their particular combination, the real question was their application to personal life problems."[192] The readings themselves define psychological understanding as a crucial part of the spiritual quest:

> The study from the human standpoint, of subconscious, subliminal, psychic, soul forces, is and should be the great study for the human family, for through self man will understand its Maker when it understands its relation to its Maker, and it will only understand that through itself, and that understanding is the knowledge as is given here in this state.[193]

Notes

Introduction

1. Edgar Cayce, *The Edgar Cayce Companion,* p. xi.

2. Thomas Sugrue, *There is a River,* p. 45.

3. Edgar Cayce, 47pp. memoirs, cited in David Bell, *Edgar Cayce's Bookshelf,* p. 20.

4. Thomas Sugrue, *There is a River,* p. 47.

5. Ibid., pp. 50–51.

6. Ibid., p. 107.

7. Ibid. Harmon Bro's biography, based on his own conversations with Cayce, does not have Edgar's parents present at this incident.

8. David M. Leary, *Edgar Cayce's Photographic Legacy,* p. 43.

9. Thomas Sugrue, *There is a River,* p. 199.

10. Ibid., p. 200.

11. Ibid., p. 202.

12. Mark Thurston and Christopher Fazel, *The Edgar Cayce Handbook for Creating Your Future,* p. 144.

13. Thomas Sugrue, *There is a River,* p. 297.

14. Harmon H. Bro, *A Seer out of Season,* p. 350.

15. A. Robert Smith, *Hugh Lynn Cayce: About My Father's Business,* pp. 219–20.

16. Ibid., p. 203.

17. Andrew Weeks, *German Mysticism from Hildegard of Bingen to Ludwig Wittgenstein,* p. 170.

1. Holistic Health Advisor

1. Reading 2263–001.

2. Reba Ann Karp, *The Edgar Cayce Encyclopedia of Healing,* p. 315.

3. Ibid., p. 520.

4. Ibid., p. 517.

5. Ibid., p. 528.

6. Edgar Cayce, *Meditation, Part II*, p. 83, reading 275–45.

7. Edgar Cayce, *The Edgar Cayce Companion*, p. 293, reading 710–1.

8. Ibid., pp. 294–95, readings 416–9, 2732–1, 1568–2, 1484–7, 340–32, 274–9, 379–10, 3316–1, 2853–1, 816–3.

9. Ibid., p. 296, reading 1013–3.

10. Ibid., p. 297, reading 540–11.

11. Ibid., reading 2602–1.

12. Ibid., reading 935–1.

13. Ibid., reading 2276–3.

14. Ibid., p. 298, reading 462–6.

15. Ibid., p. 300, reading 826–14.

16. Edgar Cayce, *Mind*, p. 159, reading 5211–7.

17. Doris Grant and Jean Joice, *Food Combining for Health*, p. 27.

18. Edgar Cayce, *The Edgar Cayce Companion*, reading 470–35.

19. Edgar Cayce, *Meditation, Part II*, p. 79, reading 3542–1.

20. Edgar Cayce, *The Edgar Cayce Companion*, reading 3511–1.

21. Ibid., p. 319, reading 759–12.

22. Ibid., p. 306, reading 480–42.

23. Ibid., p. 313, reading 584–5.

24. Ibid., p. 303, reading 1158–31.

25. Ibid., p. 309, reading 1562–1.

26. Ibid., p. 312, reading 2015–10.

27. Ibid., p. 316, readings 3121–1 and 543–26.

28. Ibid., p. 262, reading 4633–1.

29. Ibid., p. 245, reading 257–8.

30. Edgar Cayce, *On Life and Death*, p. 55, reading 257–53.

31. Sherwood Eddy, *You Will Survive Death*, pp. 96–7.

32. Ibid., p. 97.

33. Ibid., p. 99.

34. Ibid.

35. Ibid., p. 97.

36. Ibid., p. 96.

37. William McGarey, *The Edgar Cayce Remedies*, p. xi.

38. Ibid.

39. Ibid., pp. 8–9.

40. William McGarey, *The Edgar Cayce Remedies*, p. 111.

41. Ibid., p. 39.

42. Ibid., p. 76.

43. Ibid., p. 263.

44. Edgar Cayce, *The Edgar Cayce Companion*, p. 280, reading 631–4.

45. Jess Stearn, *Adventures into the Psychic*, pp. 83–4.

46. Thomas Sugrue, *There is a River*, pp. 19–22.

47. Hugh Lynn and Edgar Evans Cayce, *The Outer Limits of Edgar Cayce's Power*, pp. 23–4.

48. Thomas Sugrue, *There is a River*, pp. 19–22. C. H. Dietrich's testimonial is included among forty-two published in a promotional brochure of the Association of National Investigators, entitled "Testimony."

49. David Leary, *Edgar Cayce's Photographic Legacy*, p. 44.

50. David Kahn, *My Life with Edgar Cayce*, p. 20.

51. Edgar Cayce, *What I Believe*, p. 11.

52. Ibid., p. 29.

53. Kevin Todeschi, *Edgar Cayce's ESP*, pp. 13–16.

54. Edgar Cayce, *Psychic Development*, p. 244, reading 294–141.

55. Walter Pierpaoli and William Regelson, *The Melatonin Miracle*, pp. 34–5.

56. Edgar Cayce, *The Edgar Cayce Companion*, p. 278, reading 934–2.

57. Eric Mein, *Keys to Health*, p. xv.

58. Ibid., pp. xiii–xiv.

59. Ibid., p. xvi.

60. Martin Gardner, *Fads and Fallacies in the Name of Science*, p. 217.

61. Ibid.

62. Ibid.

63. Ibid., p. 218.

64. Edgar Evans and Hugh Lynn Cayce, *The Outer Limits of Edgar Cayce's Power*, pp. 20–22.

65. James Randi, *Flim-Flam*, p. 188.

66. Ibid., p. 189.

67. Ibid.

68. Ibid.

69. Ibid.

70. Ibid., p. 194.

71. Dale Beyerstein, "Edgar Cayce: The Prophet Who 'Slept' His Way to the Top," *Skeptical Inquirer* 20:1, January/February 1996, p. 33.

72. Edgar Cayce, *The Edgar Cayce Companion*, p. 270, reading 902–1.

73. Dale Beyerstein, "Edgar Cayce," p. 34.

74. Ibid., p. 34.

75. Ibid.

76. Ibid. Mark Thurston comments that control group research is not the sine qua non for reputable science, and that medical research (e.g., drug testing) often must rely on subjective reports. Control group research is unethical in some cases.

77. Richard Broughton, *Parapsychology*, pp. 360–61.

78. James Randi, *Flim-Flam!*, p. 195.

79. Edgar Cayce, *The Edgar Cayce Companion*, pp. 256–57, readings 120–5, 659–1.

80. Ibid., p. 254, reading 457–11.

81. Ibid., p. 285, reading 636–1.

82. Edgar Cayce, *Meditation, Part II*, p. 74, reading 2475–1.

83. Andrew Jackson Davis, *The Harmonial Philosophy*, pp. 15–25.

84. David Bell, *Edgar Cayce's Bookshelf*, p. 165.

85. Robert Ellwood, "Theosophy," in *America's Alternative Religions*, Timothy Miller, ed., p. 315.

86. Frank Podmore, *From Mesmer to Christian Science*, p. 249.

87. Ibid., pp. viii–ix.

88. Gail Harley, "New Thought and the Harmonial Family," in *America's Alternative Religions*, p. 326.

89. Edgar Cayce, *The Edgar Cayce Companion*, p. 223, reading 900–227.

90. Ibid., p. 259, reading 69–4.

91. Ibid., p. 258, reading 1967–1.

92. Ibid., reading 2528–2.

93. Ibid., p. 259, reading 281–24.

94. Edgar Cayce, *The Edgar Cayce Companion*, p. 321, reading 442–3.

95. Edgar Cayce, *Attitudes and Emotions*, Part I, p. viii. Harmon Bro argues that "attitudes and emotions" is Puryear's terminology and emphasis rather than Cayce's, but I find the volumes in the Library Series devoted to the theme persuasive in showing Puryear to base his ideas on the readings.

96. Ibid., p. xv.

97. Ibid., p. xvi, reading 5211–1.

98. Ibid., p. xvii.

99. David Bell, *Edgar Cayce's Bookshelf*, p. 221.

100. Charles Fillmore, *The Twelve Powers of Man*, p. 13.

101. Reading 2903–1.

102. H. Emilie Cady, *Lessons in Truth*, p. 56.

103. Reading 3460–1.

104. Edgar Cayce, *The Edgar Cayce Companion*, p. 353, reading 397–1.

105. Edgar Cayce, *What is Truth*, p. 25.

106. David Bell, personal letter, October 15, 1996.

107. Ibid.

108. Phillip Lucas, "The Association for Research and Enlightenment," *America's Alternative Religions*, p. 356.

109. Ibid., p. 357.

110. Ibid.

111. Reading 1436–1.

112. J. Gordon Melton, "Whither the New Age?" *America's Alternative Religions*, p. 349.

113. Phillip Lucas, "The Association for Research and Enlightenment," *America's Alternative Religions,* p. 356; Mark Thurston, personal correspondence 7/1/97.

114. Isadore Rosenfeld, *Dr. Rosenfeld's Guide to Alternative Medicine,* pp. xx–xxi.

115. Ibid., p. xxi.

2. Christian Theosopher

1. Antoine Faivre, *Access to Western Esotericism,* p. 23.

2. Ibid., p. 19.

3. Ibid., p. 27.

4. Ibid., pp. 31–2.

5. Arthur Versluis, *Theosophia,* p. 13.

6. Ibid., p. 27.

7. Edgar Cayce, *Life and Death,* p. 61, reading 1460–2.

8. Ibid., p. 63, reading 1567–2.

9. Edgar Cayce, *Study Group Readings,* reading 262–12.

10. Edgar Cayce, *Life and Death,* p. 66, reading 263–13.

11. Ibid., p. 127, reading 5749–3.

12. Edgar Cayce, *Psychic Development,* p. 98, reading 5752–3.

13. Ibid., p. 99.

14. Ibid.

15. Edgar Cayce, *Life and Death,* p. 85, reading 1662–1.

16. Ibid., p. 127, reading 5749–3.

17. Edgar Cayce, *Early Christian Epoch,* p. 137, reading 2067–7.

18. Ibid., p. 131, reading 364–7.

19. Edgar Cayce, *Life and Death,* p. 115, reading 849–18.

20. Ibid., p. 128, reading 5749–3.

21. Reading 2067–2.

22. Edgar Cayce, *Meditation, Vol. I,* p. 183, reading 281–34.

23. Ibid., p. 208, reading 281–40.

24. Edgar Cayce, *Study Group Readings,* p. 65, reading 262–14.

25. Ibid., p. 169, reading 262–40.

26. Ibid., p. 299, reading 262–75.

27. Ibid., p. 179, reading 262–44.

28. Ibid., p. 229, reading 262–58.

29. Ibid., p. 246, reading 262–61.

30. *The Guideposts Parallel Bible,* p. 2740.

31. Ibid., p. 2742.

32. Ibid.

33. Ibid., p. 2744.

34. Ibid., p. 2750.

35. D. Moody Smith, *The Theology of the Gospel of John,* p. 24.

36. H. P. Blavatsky, *The Key to Theosophy,* p. 187.

37. Edgar Cayce, *Psychic Awareness,* p. 345, reading 4087–1.

38. Edgar Cayce, *Jesus the Pattern,* p. 86, reading 272–9.

39. *The Guideposts Parallel Bible,* pp. 540–42.

40. *New Bible Commentary,* p. 226.

41. Edgar Cayce, *Meditation, Part Two,* p. 99, reading 1861–11.

42. Ibid., p. 142, reading 707–2.

43. Edgar Cayce, *Meditation: Part Two,* p. 34, reading 470–10.

44. Ibid., p. 129, reading 282–3.

45. Edgar Cayce, *Dreams and Dreaming, Part II,* p. 671, reading 900–103.

46. Ibid., p. 711, reading 900–127.

47. Ibid., p. 753, reading 900–156.

48. Ibid., p. 821, reading 900–202.

49. Harmon Bro, *A Seer Out of Season,* p. 325.

50. Thomas Sugrue, *There is a River,* p. 297.

51. Edgar Cayce, *Psychic Development,* p. 116, reading 254–83.

52. Ibid.

53. Ibid.

54. Ibid., p. 117.

55. Ibid., pp. 117–18.

56. Ibid., p. 119, reading 440–8.

57. Edgar Cayce, *The Early Christian Epoch*, p. 103, reading 1010–17.

58. Edgar Cayce, *Psychic Development*, p. 118, reading 254–109.

59. Ibid., p. 120, reading 845–1.

60. Ibid., reading 845–6.

61. Ibid., p. 121, reading 1152–11.

62. Ibid., pp. 121–22, reading 3011–3.

63. Edgar Cayce, *The Edgar Cayce Companion*, p. 228, reading 5749–14.

64. Edgar Cayce, *Christ Consciousness*, p. 56, reading 5749–4.

65. Edgar Cayce, *Christ Consciousness*, p. 19, reading 137–127.

66. Ibid., p. 97, reading 696–3.

67. Ibid., pp. 164–65, reading 1158–14.

68. Ibid., p. 250, reading 3285–2.

69. Edgar Cayce, *Jesus the Pattern*, p. 296, reading 3054–4.

70. Ibid., p. 201, reading 2067–2.

71. Ibid., p. 300, reading 4071–1.

72. Edgar Cayce, *Soul Development*, p. 150, reading 5030–1.

73. Edgar Cayce, *Jesus the Pattern*, p. 63, reading 254–71.

74. Ibid., p. 115, reading 1152–4.

75. Ibid., p. 185, reading 1971–1.

76. Ibid., p. 191, reading 2067–1.

77. Edgar Cayce, *Psychic Development*, p. 119, reading 587–6.

78. Harmon Bro, *A Seer Out of Season*, p. 287.

79. Ibid., p. 342.

80. Ibid., p. 347.

81. Ibid., p. 125.

82. Ibid., p. 27.

83. Arthur Ford, *Nothing So Strange*, p. 171.

84. Harmon Bro, *The Charisma of the Seer*, p. 36.

85. David Bell, *Edgar Cayce's Bookshelf,* p. 166.

86. Ibid., p. 166.

87. Harmon Bro, *Charisma of the Seer,* p. 136.

88. Stephen Prothero, *The White Buddhist,* p. 7.

89. Ibid., p. 8.

90. Harmon Bro, *A Seer Out of Season,* p. 353.

91. David Bell, personal letter, October 15, 1996.

92. David Bell, *Edgar Cayce's Bookshelf,* p. 212, reading 2155–2 correspondence.

93. Ibid., p. 221.

94. Harmon Bro, *The Charisma of the Seer,* p. 36.

95. Ibid., p. 98.

96. Ibid., p. 49.

97. David Bell, *Edgar Cayce's Bookshelf,* p. 193.

98. Ibid., p. 194.

99. Reading 8311–6.

100. Reading 1152–1.

101. Reading 954–24.

102. Reading 10311–006.

103. Edgar Cayce, *Meditation: Part II,* p. 169, reading 1742–4.

104. Edgar Cayce, *Dreams and Dreaming, Vol. I,* p. 391, reading 294–126.

105. Ibid., p. 440, reading 294–196.

106. Peter Berger, *A Rumor of Angels,* p. 42.

107. Ibid., p. 43.

108. Peter Berger, *The Heretical Imperative,* pp. 66–156.

109. Edgar Cayce, *Soul Development,* p. 258, reading 5392–1.

110. Harmon Bro, *The Charisma of the Seer,* p. 162.

111. Ibid., p. 165.

112. Harold Bloom, *The American Religion,* p. 17.

113. Ibid., p. 31.

114. Edgar Cayce, *Mind,* p. 139, reading 524–2.

115. Edgar Cayce, *Soul Development,* p. 106, reading 1096–4.

116. Ibid., p. 109, reading 2003–1.

117. Edgar Cayce, 21, p. 107, reading 1096–4.

118. Harold Bloom, *The American Religion*, p. 32.

119. Ibid., p. 264.

120. Edgar Cayce, *Soul Development*, p. 113, reading 2079–1.

121. Ibid.

122. Burton Mack, *Who Wrote the New Testament?*, p. 175.

123. Richard Henry Drummond, *A Life of Jesus the Christ*, p. 116.

124. Ibid., p. xiii.

125. Ibid., p. 195.

126. Richard Henry Drummond, *Unto the Churches*, p. 72.

127. Ibid., pp. 72–3.

3. Clairvoyant Time Traveler

1. Edgar Evans Cayce, *Edgar Cayce on Atlantis*, p. 82.

2. Edgar Cayce, *The Edgar Cayce Companion*, p. 49, reading 254–47.

3. Ibid., p. 57, reading 2533–8.

4. Robert Krajenke, *From the Birth of Souls to the Death of Moses*, p. 9, reading 364–10.

5. Edgar Cayce, *Atlantis*, p. 13, reading 364–9.

6. Edgar Cayce, *Soul Development*, p. 14, reading 3744–4.

7. Robert Krajenke, *From the Birth of Souls to the Death of Moses*, p. 49, reading 900–227.

8. Edgar Cayce, *The Edgar Cayce Reader*, p. 393, reading 5748–2.

9. Edgar Cayce, *The Edgar Cayce Companion*, p. 371, reading 364–1.

10. Edgar Evans Cayce, *Edgar Cayce on Atlantis*, p. 27.

11. H. P. Blavatsky, *The Secret Doctrine*, Vol. II, pp. 423–33.

12. Edgar Cayce, *Atlantis*, p. 15, reading 3579–1.

13. Ibid., p. 26, reading 275–38.

14. Ibid., p. 28, reading 5257–1.

15. Ibid., p. 22, reading 187–1.

16. Ibid., p. 21, reading 428–4.

17. Edgar Cayce, *The Edgar Cayce Companion*, p. 381, reading 2464–2.

18. Edgar Cayce, *Atlantis*, p. 30, reading 877–26.

19. Ibid., p. 32, reading 884–1.

20. Edgar Cayce, *The Edgar Cayce Companion*, p. 376, reading 364–6.

21. Edgar Cayce, *Atlantis*, p. 41, readings 470–22, 470–33.

22. Ibid., p. 43, reading 364–6.

23. Ibid., pp. 45–6, readings 877–26 and 440–5.

24. Ibid., pp. 46–7, reading 440–5.

25. Edgar Cayce, *The Edgar Cayce Companion*, p. 387, reading 2072–10.

26. Ibid., p. 363, reading 2562–1.

27. Ibid., p. 389, reading 519–1.

28. Ibid., pp. 390–91, reading 262–39.

29. Edgar Cayce, *Atlantis*, p. 24, reading 364–11.

30. Ibid., p. 24, reading 364–4.

31. Ibid., p. 16, reading 364–4.

32. Edgar Cayce, *The Edgar Cayce Companion*, p. 430, reading 3528–1.

33. Ibid., p. 391, reading 1211–1.

34. Ibid., p. 371, reading 364–3.

35. Edgar Evans Cayce, *Edgar Cayce on Atlantis*, p. 18.

36. Lytle Robinson, *Edgar Cayce's Story of the Origin and Destiny of Man*, p. 75.

37. Ibid., p. 77.

38. Edgar Cayce, *The Edgar Cayce Companion*, p. 408, reading 2072–10.

39. Ibid., p. 404, reading 1223–4.

40. Lytle Robinson, *Edgar Cayce's Story of the Origin and Destiny of Man*, p. 80.

41. Edgar Cayce, *The Edgar Cayce Companion*, p. 403, reading 275–33.

42. Ibid., p. 405, reading 281–25.

43. Lytle Robinson, *Edgar Cayce's Story of the Origin and Destiny of Man*, p. 81.

44. Ibid., p. 83.

45. Edgar Cayce, *The Edgar Cayce Companion,* p. 410, reading 315–4.

46. Lytle Robinson, *Edgar Cayce's Story of the Origin and Destiny of Man,* p. 88.

47. Ibid., p. 89.

48. Ibid.

49. Edgar Cayce, *The Edgar Cayce Companion,* p. 415, reading 5748–6.

50. Ibid., p. 399, reading 294–148.

51. Mark Lehner, "The Search for Ra Ta" (Interview by A. Robert Smith), *Venture Inward* I:3, January/February 1986, p. 6.

52. Ibid., p. 7.

53. Ibid., p. 8.

54. Ibid., p. 9.

55. Ibid.

56. Ibid., p. 47.

57. Mark Lehner, "Ra Ta: Myth or Reality?" *Venture Inward* 1:4, March/April 1986, p. 6.

58. Ibid., p. 7.

59. Ibid., p. 8.

60. Ibid.

61. Ibid., p. 9.

62. Ibid.

63. Ibid., p. 10.

64. Ibid., p. 11.

65. Ibid., pp. 12–13.

66. William Fix *et al.,* "Keep Digging for Ra Ta," *Venture Inward* 2:6, November/December 1986, p. 47.

67. A. Robert Smith, *Hugh Lynn Cayce: About My Father's Business,* p. 246.

68. Ibid., p. 250.

69. Ibid., p. 253.

70. Ibid., p. 248.

71. Richard Heinberg, "The Lost History of Mankind," *Venture Inward* 12:3, May/June 1996, p. 31.

72. Ibid., p. 32.

73. Ibid., p. 34.

74. Robert M. Schoch, "The Sphinx: Older by Half?" (Interview), *Venture Inward* 8:1, January/February 1992, p. 148.

75. Edgar Cayce, *The Edgar Cayce Companion*, p. 219, reading 2067–11.

76. James H. Charlesworth, *Jesus and the Dead Sea Scrolls*, p. xvii.

77. Ibid., p. 2.

78. Ibid., p. 38.

79. David Bell, personal letter, October 15, 1996.

80. David Bell, *Edgar Cayce's Bookshelf*, p. 165.

81. Ibid., p. 231.

82. Ibid., pp. 289–90.

83. Ibid., pp. 294–96.

84. Marcus Borg, *Meeting Jesus Again for the First Time*, p. 30.

85. Ibid., pp. 2–3.

86. Edgar Cayce, *Soul Development*, p. 127, reading 488–6.

87. Edgar Cayce, *Jesus the Pattern*, p. 194, reading 2081–1.

88. *The Guideposts Parallel Bible*, p. 2560.

89. Edgar Cayce, *Jesus the Pattern*, p. 240, reading 357–13.

90. Jacques Barzun and Henry Graff, *The Modern Researcher*, pp. 174–75.

91. David Bell, *Edgar Cayce's Bookshelf*, p. 266.

92. Ibid., p. 267.

93. Ibid., p. 270.

94. Ibid., p. 315.

95. Ibid.

96. Edgar Cayce, *Soul Development*, p. 181, reading 538–9.

97. Harmon Bro, *The Charisma of the Seer*, p. 144.

98. Jeffrey Furst, *The Return of Frances Willard*, p. 156.

99. Edgar Cayce, *The Edgar Cayce Companion*, p. 246, reading 2067–1.

100. Mark Thurston, *Visions and Prophecies of a New Age*, p. 18.

101. Ibid., p. 19.

102. Ibid., p. 350, reading 2533–4.

103. Ibid., p. 5, reading 1472–14.

104. Edgar Cayce, *Psychic Development*, p. 215, reading 294–8.

105. Edgar Cayce, *Psychic Awareness*, p. 364, reading 5751–1.

106. Edgar Cayce, *The Edgar Cayce Companion*, p. 136, reading 3162–1.

107. Ibid., p. 431, reading 2665–2.

108. Ibid., p. 5, reading 254–2.

109. Ibid., p. 2, reading 288–27.

110. Gina Cerminara, *Many Mansions*, p. 37.

111. Gregory Tillett, *The Elder Brother*, pp. 119–20.

112. Paul Edwards, *Reincarnation*, pp. 225–26.

113. Erik Youngberg, "A Reincarnation Theory Dilemma," *The New Millennium* 1:2, October/November 1996, p. 27.

114. Paul Edwards, *Reincarnation*, p. 279.

115. Carl B. Becker, *Paranormal Experience and Survival of Death*, p. 188.

116. Edgar Cayce, *The Edgar Cayce Companion*, p. 445, reading 270–30.

117. Ibid., p. 444, reading 3976–15.

118. Ibid.

119. Ibid., p. 416, reading 5748–6.

120. Ibid., p. 442, reading 3976–15.

121. Ibid., p. 441, reading 900–272.

122. Ibid., p. 445, reading 1152–11.

123. Ibid., p. 449, reading 1152–11.

124. Ibid., pp. 446–47, readings 311–8, 311–10.

125. Ibid., p. 416, reading 5748–6.

126. Ibid., p. 424, reading 2329–3.

127. Ibid., p. 376, reading 364–11.

128. Ibid., p. 416, reading 5748–6.

129. Ibid., p. 448, reading 2378–16.

130. Ibid., p. 448, reading 2976–15.

131. Ibid., p. 444, reading 958–3.

132. Ibid., pp. 338–39, reading 440–5.

133. Douglas Richards, "Did Atlanteans Build the First Pentagon?," *Venture Inward* 2:2, March/April 1986, p. 21.

134. Edgar Cayce, *The Edgar Cayce Companion,* p. 441, reading 2780–3.

135. Ibid., reading 3976–19.

136. Ibid., p. 440, reading 3976–24.

137. Ibid., p. 439, reading 3976–29.

138. Ibid., p. 231, reading 5749–5.

139. Ibid., p. 444, reading 1602–3.

140. Ibid., p. 160, reading 1602–3.

141. Edgar Evans Cayce, *Edgar Cayce on Atlantis,* pp. 28–9.

142. Reading 3902–2.

143. Reading 5281–1.

144. Edgar Cayce, *The Edgar Cayce Companion,* p. 232, reading 5749–4.

145. Ibid., p. 233, reading 1152–1.

146. Ibid., p. 345, reading 281–16.

147. Ibid., p. 439, reading 452–5.

148. Ibid., p. 419, reading 5748–6.

149. Ibid., p. 422, reading 378–14.

150. Ibid., pp. 442–43, reading 3976–15.

151. Edgar Evans Cayce, *Edgar Cayce on Atlantis,* p. 161.

152. Martin Ebon, *Prophecy in Our Time,* p. 38.

153. Ibid., p. 39.

154. Ibid., p. 42.

155. Edgar Evans and Hugh Lynn Cayce, *The Outer Limits of Edgar Cayce's Power,* p. 31.

156. Douglas Richards, "Did Atlanteans Build the First Pentagon?," *Venture Inward* 2:2, March/April 1986, p. 24, reading 245–88.

157. Ibid., reading 254–95.

158. Harmon Bro, *The Charisma of the Seer,* p. 144.

159. David Bell, *Edgar Cayce's Bookshelf,* p. 318.

160. Mark Thurston, *Visions and Prophecies for a New Age,* p. 26.

161. Mark Thurston, personal communication, July 1, 1997.

162. Ibid.

163. Richard Drummond, *A Life of Jesus the Christ,* p. xx.

164. Mark Thurston, personal communication, July 1, 1997.

165. Ibid.

166. A. Robert Smith, "Lessons from Heaven's Gate," *Venture Inward* 13:4, July/August 1997, p. 58.

167. A. Robert Smith, "Schor Claims Discovery of 'Huge Room' Beneath Sphinx," *Venture Inward* 13:5, September/October 1997, p. 5.

168. Ibid.

4. Esoteric Psychologist

1. Antoine Faivre, *Access to Western Esotericism,* pp. 10–13.

2. Edgar Cayce, *Astrology, Part I,* p. 541, reading 2771–1.

3. Edgar Cayce, *Mind,* p. 186, reading 416–10.

4. Ibid., p. 55, reading 1822–1.

5. Edgar Cayce, *The Study Group Readings,* p. 32, reading 262–8.

6. Edgar Cayce, *Mind,* pp. 10–11, reading 3744–1.

7. Edgar Cayce, *Christ Consciousness,* p. 155, reading 987–4.

8. Edgar Cayce, *The Edgar Cayce Companion,* p. 43, reading 262–80.

9. Edgar Cayce, *Christ Consciousness,* p. 187, reading 1646–7.

10. Edgar Cayce, *The Edgar Cayce Companion,* p. 84, reading 1885–1.

11. Ibid., p. 83, reading 262–123.

12. Ibid., p. 83, reading 4083–1.

13. Ibid., p. 86, reading 2533–8.

14. Edgar Cayce, *Dreams and Dreaming, Part II,* p. 591, reading 1595–1.

15. Herbert Puryear, *The Edgar Cayce Primer,* pp. 66–7.

16. Carl Jung, *The Portable Jung,* p. 142.

17. Edgar Cayce, *Mind,* p. 94, reading 696–3.

18. Ibid.

19. Edgar Cayce, *The Edgar Cayce Companion*, p. 37, reading 2995–1.

20. Ibid., p. 37, reading 345–2.

21. Ibid., reading 3211–2.

22. George I. Gurdjieff, *Views from the Real World*, p. 143.

23. Edgar Cayce, *The Edgar Cayce Companion*, p. 80, reading 3744–1.

24. Ibid., pp. 80–81, reading 900–31.

25. Ibid., p. 82, reading 900–21.

26. Edgar Cayce, *Mind*, p. 211, reading 2475–1.

27. Edgar Cayce, *Life and Death*, p. 23, reading 1755–3.

28. Ibid., p. 72, reading 274–3.

29. Ibid., p. 86, reading 307–3.

30. Ibid., p. 100, reading 845–4.

31. Carl Jung, *The Portable Jung*, p. 145.

32. Ibid., p. 146.

33. Edgar Cayce, *The Edgar Cayce Companion*, p. 44, reading 2074–1.

34. Herbert Puryear and Mark Thurston, *Meditation and the Mind of Man*, p. 75.

35. Edgar Cayce, *Soul Development*, p. 147, reading 1538–1.

36. Ibid., p. 147, reading 2056–2.

37. Edgar Cayce, *The Edgar Cayce Companion*, p. 40, reading 900–357.

38. Mark Thurston and Christopher Fazel, *The Edgar Cayce Handbook for Creating Your Future*, p. 15.

39. George I. Gurdjieff, *Views From the Real World*, p. 148.

40. Edgar Cayce, *Mind*, p. 132, reading 1977–1.

41. Edgar Cayce, *The Edgar Cayce Companion*, p. 32, reading 1538–1.

42. Edgar Cayce, *Daily Living*, p. 219, reading 826–6.

43. Ibid., p. 218.

44. Ibid., p. 229, reading 5747–3.

45. Edgar Cayce, *Psychic Development*, p. 153, reading 1089–2.

46. Harmon Bro, *A Seer Out of Season*, p. 2.

47. Harmon Bro, *The Charisma of the Seer*, p. 140.

48. David Bell, personal correspondence, October 15, 1996.

49. Harmon Bro, *A Seer Out of Season,* p. 158.

50. Reading 136–059.

51. Harmon Bro, *The Charisma of the Seer,* p. 46.

52. Ibid., p. 129.

53. Harmon Bro, *The Charisma of the Seer,* p. 46.

54. Ibid., p. 78.

55. Ibid., pp. 81–2.

56. Harmon Bro, *A Seer Out of Season,* p. 3.

57. Ibid., p. 16.

58. Harmon Bro, *The Charisma of the Seer,* pp. 5–6.

59. Ibid.

60. Ibid., p. 30.

61. Ibid., p. 34.

62. Joseph LeDoux, *The Emotional Brain,* pp. 29–32, 55–64.

63. Edgar Cayce, *The Edgar Cayce Companion,* p. 121, reading 1152–12.

64. Ibid., p. 124, reading 2982–2.

65. Ibid., p. 35, reading 900–24.

66. Ibid., p. 131, reading 314–1.

67. Edgar Cayce, *Christ Consciousness,* p. 181, reading 1567–2.

68. Edgar Cayce, *Mind,* p. 211, reading 1650–1.

69. Edgar Cayce, *The Edgar Cayce Companion,* p. 140, reading 100–10.

70. Edgar Cayce, *On Life and Death,* p. 76, reading 541–7.

71. Edgar Cayce, *Psychic Development,* p. 173, reading 2823–1.

72. Edgar Cayce, *Mind,* p. 288, reading 311–2.

73. Edgar Cayce, *Astrology, Part I,* p. 546, reading 3006–1.

74. Edgar Cayce, *Mind,* p. 287, reading 311–2.

75. Edgar Cayce, *Mind,* p. 270, reading 1523–4.

76. Ibid., p. 278, reading 1353–1.

77. Ibid., p. 284, reading 2533–1.

78. Edgar Cayce, *Astrology, Part I,* p. 537, reading 2594–1.

79. G. de Purucker, *Dialogues of G. de Purucker*, vol. III, p. 398.

80. Edgar Cayce, *Astrology, Part I*, pp. 549–50, reading 3376–1.

81. Margaret Gammon, *Astrology in the Edgar Cayce Readings*, pp. 3, 5.

82. Hans Eysenck and D. K. B. Nias, *Astrology: Science or Superstition?*, pp. 220–21.

83. Ibid., p. 219.

84. Ibid.

85. David Bell, *Edgar Cayce's Bookshelf*, p. 195.

86. Rudolf Steiner, *Life Between Death and Rebirth*, p. 39.

87. Edgar Cayce, *Dreams and Dreaming, Part II*, p. 1109, reading 4167–1.

88. Edgar Cayce, *Jesus the Pattern*, p. 118, reading 262–104.

89. H. P. Blavatsky, *Transactions of the Blavatsky Lodge*, p. 79.

90. Harmon Bro, *Edgar Cayce on Dreams*, pp. 17–19.

91. Carl Jung, *The Portable Jung*, pp. 76–7.

92. Edgar Cayce, *Dreams and Dreaming, Part I*, pp. 395, reading 294–131.

93. David Bell, personal letter, October 15, 1996.

94. Robert Wuthnow, *Christianity in the 21st Century*, p. 215.

95. *A Search for God, Book I*, p. 22, reading 262–3.

96. Mark Thurston and Christopher Fazel, *The Edgar Cayce Handbook for Creating Your Future*, pp. 17, 179–80.

97. Worth Kidd, *Edgar Cayce and Group Dynamics*, p. 20.

98. *The Handbook for A.R.E. Study Groups*, pp. 22–4.

99. Ibid., p. 37, reading 254–15.

100. Ibid., p. 5.

101. Edgar Cayce, *The Edgar Cayce Companion*, p. 2, reading 294–1.

102. Ibid., p. 243, reading 307–4.

103. David Bell, *Edgar Cayce's Bookshelf*, p. 172.

104. Harmon Bro, *The Charisma of the Seer*, p. 164.

105. Edgar Cayce, "What is Truth?," *The Edgar Cayce Reader*, pp. 30–31.

106. Harmon Bro, *A Seer Out of Season*, p. 272.

107. Edgar Cayce, "What is Truth?," *The Edgar Cayce Reader*, p. 33.

108. Gina Cerminara, *Edgar Cayce Revisited and Other Candid Commentaries*, p. 119.

109. Thomas Sugrue, *There is a River*, p. 15.

110. Martin Gardner, *Fads and Fallacies In the Name of Science*, p. 218.

111. Edgar Cayce, *Mind*, p. 84, reading 3605–1.

112. Edgar Cayce, *The Edgar Cayce Companion*, p. 7, reading 254–67.

113. Henry Reed, *Edgar Cayce on Channeling Your Higher Self*, p. 178.

114. Edgar Cayce, *Christ Consciousness*, p. 220, reading 2630–1.

115. Ibid., p. 62, reading 422–1.

116. Edgar Cayce, *Psychic Development*, p. 128, reading 1265–3.

117. Edgar Cayce, *Auras*, p. 1.

118. Ibid.

119. Ibid., p. 20.

120. Edgar Cayce, *Meditation, Part I*, p. 67, reading 281–13.

121. Edgar Cayce, *Psychic Development*, p. 234, reading 1782–1.

122. Mark Juergensmeyer, *Radhasoami Reality*, p. 97.

123. Ibid., p. 101.

124. Ibid.

125. Edgar Cayce, *Psychic Development*, p. 241, reading 826–11.

126. Ibid., p. 136, reading 540–3.

127. Edgar Cayce, *The Edgar Cayce Companion*, p. 69, reading 987–4.

128. Ibid., p. 107, reading 462–8.

129. H. P. Blavatsky, *The Voice of the Silence*, p. 9.

130. Shiv Dayal Singh, *Sar Bachan*, p. 55.

131. Edgar Cayce, *The Edgar Cayce Companion*, p. 56, reading 136–83.

132. Edgar Cayce, *Psychic Development*, p. 312, reading 5754–7.

133. Shiv Dayal Singh, *Sar Bachan*, p. 35.

134. Edgar Cayce, *Psychic Development*, p. 236, reading 5286–1.

135. Edgar Cayce, *Psychic Awareness*, p. 10, reading 922–1.

136. David Bell, *Edgar Cayce's Bookshelf*, p. 226.

137. Ibid., p. 227, reading 2067–4.

138. Ibid., pp. 238–39.

139. Reading 900–89.

140. Edgar Cayce, *Psychic Development,* p. 84, reading 294–40.

141. Henry Reed, *Edgar Cayce on Channeling Your Higher Self,* p. 103.

142. Jeffrey Furst, *Edgar Cayce's Story of Attitudes and Emotions,* p. 84.

143. Edgar Cayce, *Meditation, Part II,* p. 192, reading 294–142.

144. H. P. Blavatsky, *Inner Group Teachings of H. P. Blavatsky,* p. 25.

145. Ibid., p. 135.

146. Ibid., p. 176.

147. Edgar Cayce, *The Edgar Cayce Companion,* p. 64, reading 261–14.

148. Henri Corbin, *Man of Light in Iranian Sufism,* p. 125.

149. Ibid., pp. 127, 129.

150. Edgar Cayce, *The Edgar Cayce Companion,* pp. 69–70, reading 987–4.

151. Edgar Cayce, *Psychic Development,* p. 264, reading 5392–1.

152. Edgar Cayce, *Psychic Awareness,* p. 83, reading 254–87.

153. Reading 255–12.

154. Andrea Diem, *Shabdism in North America,* p. 134.

155. Ibid., pp. 134–35.

156. David C. Lane, *Making of a Spiritual Movement,* online edition, "The New Panths," p. 2.

157. Ibid., p. 8.

158. Andrea Diem, *Shabdism in North America,* p. 135.

159. Ibid.

160. Bhagat Singh Thind, *House of Happiness,* p. 218.

161. Ibid., p. 222.

162. Ibid., pp. 190, 192.

163. Ibid., pp. 198–99.

164. Ibid., p. 211.

165. Bhagat Singh Thind, *Science of Union With God Here and Now,* p. 212.

166. Andrea Diem, *Shabdism in North America,* p. 139.

167. Ibid., p. 149.

168. Reading 866–1.

169. Ibid.

170. Reading 873–1.

171. Reading 866–1.

172. Ibid.

173. Ibid.

174. Reading 873–1.

175. Reading 989–1.

176. Reading 813–1.

177. Reading 866–1.

178. Ibid.

179. Ibid.

180. Ibid.

181. A. Robert Smith, *About My Father's Business*, p. 231.

182. I. C. Sharma, *Cayce, Karma and Reincarnation*, p. xii.

183. Andrea Diem, *Shabdism in North America*, p. 45.

184. David C. Lane, personal correspondence, 7/17/97.

185. Reading 813–1.

186. Sidney Rosen, "One Thousand Induction Techniques and Their Application to Therapy and Thinking," *Ericksonian Methods*, pp. 333–34.

187. Ronald Numbers, *Prophetess of Health*, p. 84.

188. Ibid., p. 194.

189. Richard S. Broughton, *Parapsychology*, p. 140.

190. Ibid., p. 4.

191. Ibid., p. 80.

192. Harmon Bro, *The Charisma of the Seer*, p. 172.

193. Edgar Cayce, *The Edgar Cayce Companion*, p. iii, reading 3744–4.

Bibliography

Agee, Doris. *Edgar Cayce on ESP.* New York: Castle, 1969.

Bailey, Alice A. *The Unfinished Autobiography of Alice A. Bailey.* New York: Lucis, 1951.

Barzun, Jacques, and Henry F. Graff. *The Modern Researcher.* 4th ed. New York: Harcourt Brace College Publications, 1985.

Becker, Carl B. *Paranormal Experience and Survival of Death.* Albany: State University of New York Press, 1993.

Bell, David. *Edgar Cayce's Bookshelf.* Unpublished Ph.D. dissertation, California Institute of Integral Studies.

Berger, Peter. *The Heretical Imperative.* Garden City, N.Y.: Anchor/Doubleday, 1979.

———. *A Rumor of Angels.* Garden City, N.Y.: Anchor/Doubleday, 1969.

Bernstein, Morey. *The Search for Bridey Murphy.* Garden City, N.Y.: Doubleday, 1956.

Beyerstein, Dale. "Edgar Cayce: The 'Prophet' who 'Slept' His Way to the Top." *Skeptical Inquirer* 20:1 (January-February 1996), pp. 32–37.

Blavatsky, H. P. *The Inner Group Teachings of H. P. Blavatsky.* San Diego: Point Loma, 1995.

———. *The Key to Theosophy.* Los Angeles: Theosophy Company, 1974.

———. *The Secret Doctrine.* Los Angeles: Theosophy Company, 1974.

———. *Transactions of the Blavatsky Lodge of the Theosophical Society.* Los Angeles: Theosophy Company, 1923.

Bloom, Harold J. *The American Religion.* New York: Simon & Schuster, 1992.

Borg, Marcus J. *Meeting Jesus Again for the First Time.* San Francisco: Harper, 1994.

Bro, Harmon H. *The Charisma of the Seer.* Ph.D. dissertation, University of Chicago, 1955.

———. *Edgar Cayce on Dreams.* New York: Warner, 1968.

———. *A Seer Out of Season.* New York: Harper & Row, 1989.

Broughton, Richard S. *Parapsychology: The Controversial Science.* New York: Ballantine, 1991.

Cady, H. Emilie. *How I Used Truth.* Unity Village, Mo.: Unity School of Christianity, n.d.

Cayce, Edgar. *Astrology, Part 1.* Virginia Beach: A.R.E., 1985. (The Edgar Cayce Readings, vol. 18)

———. *Astrology, Part 2.* Virginia Beach: A.R.E., 1985. (The Edgar Cayce Readings, vol. 19)

———. *Atlantis.* Virginia Beach: A.R.E., 1987. (The Edgar Cayce Readings, vol. 22)

———. *Attitudes and Emotions, Part 1.* Virginia Beach: A.R.E., 1981. (The Edgar Cayce Readings, vol. 13)

———. *Attitudes and Emotions, Part 2.* Virginia Beach: A.R.E., 1982. (The Edgar Cayce Readings, vol. 14)

———. *Attitudes and Emotions, Part 3.* Virginia Beach: A.R.E., 1982. (The Edgar Cayce Readings, vol. 15)

———. *Auras.* Virginia Beach: A.R.E., 1973.

———. *Christ Consciousness.* Virginia Beach: A.R.E., 1980. (The Edgar Cayce Readings, vol. 11)

———. *Daily Living: Meeting Life's Challenges.* Virginia Beach: A.R.E., 1981. (The Edgar Cayce Readings, vol. 12)

———. *Dreams and Dreaming, Part I.* Virginia Beach: A.R.E., 1976. (The Edgar Cayce Readings, vol. 4)

———. *Dreams and Dreaming, Part II.* Virginia Beach: A.R.E., 1976. (The Edgar Cayce Readings, vol. 5)

———. *The Early Christian Epoch.* Virginia Beach: A.R.E., 1976. (The Edgar Cayce Readings, vol. 6)

———. *The Edgar Cayce Companion.* R. Ernest Frejer, compiler. Virginia Beach: A.R.E., 1995.

———. *The Edgar Cayce Reader.* New York: Paperback Library, 1969.

———. *Egypt at the Time of Ra Ta, Part I: The Story of Ra Ta.* Virginia Beach: A.R.E., 1989. (The Edgar Cayce Readings, vol. 23)

———. *Egypt at the Time of Ra Ta, Part II: The Teachings and the Temples.* Virginia Beach: A.R.E., 1989. (The Edgar Cayce Readings, vol. 24.)

———. *The Expanded Search for God, Part I.* Virginia Beach: A.R.E., 1983. (The Edgar Cayce Readings, vol. 16)

———. *The Expanded Search for God, Part II.* Virginia Beach: A.R.E., 1983. (The Edgar Cayce Readings, vol. 17)

———. *Jesus the Pattern.* Virginia Beach: A.R.E., 1980. (The Edgar Cayce Readings, vol. 10)

———. *Meditation, Part I: Healing, Prayer, and the Revelation.* Virginia Beach: A.R.E., 1974. (The Edgar Cayce Readings, vol. 2)

———. *Meditation, Part II: Meditation, Endocrine Glands, Prayer, and Affirmations.* Virginia Beach: A.R.E., 1975. (The Edgar Cayce Readings, vol. 3)

———. *Mind.* Virginia Beach: A.R.E., 1986. (The Edgar Cayce Readings, vol. 20)

———. *On Life and Death.* Virginia Beach: A.R.E., 1973. (The Edgar Cayce Readings, vol. 1)

———. *Psychic Awareness.* Virginia Beach: A.R.E., 1979. (The Edgar Cayce Readings, vol. 9)

———. *Psychic Development.* Virginia Beach: A.R.E., 1978. (The Edgar Cayce Readings, vol. 8)

———. *Soul Development.* Virginia Beach: A.R.E., 1986. (The Edgar Cayce Readings, vol. 21)

———. *The Study Group Readings.* Virginia Beach: A.R.E., 1977. (The Edgar Cayce Readings, vol. 7)

———. *What I Believe.* Virginia Beach: A.R.E., n.d.

Cayce, Edgar Evans. *Edgar Cayce on Atlantis.* New York: Warner, 1968.

Cayce, Edgar Evans and Hugh Lynn. *The Outer Limits of Edgar Cayce's Power.* New York: Bell, 1971.

Cerminara, Gina. *Edgar Cayce Revisited and Other Candid Commentaries.* Norfolk: Unilaw, 1983.

———. *Many Mansions.* New York: NAL, 1967.

Charlesworth, James H. *Jesus and the Dead Sea Scrolls.* New York: Doubleday, 1993.

Church, W. H. *Edgar Cayce's Story of the Soul.* Virginia Beach: A.R.E., 1989.

———. *The Lives of Edgar Cayce.* Virginia Beach: A.R.E., 1995.

Corbin, Henri. *The Man of Light in Iranian Sufism.* Boulder: Shambhala, 1978.

Crossan, John Dominic. *Jesus: A Revolutionary Biography.* San Francisco: Harper, 1994.

Curry, Patrick, Nicholas Campion, and Jacques Halbronn. *La Vie Astrologique il y a Cent Ans.* Paris: La Grande Conjonction, 1992.

Davis, Andrew Jackson. *The Harmonial Philosophy.* Milwaukee: National Spiritual Association of Churches, n.d.

Diem, Andrea. *Shabdism in North America: The Influence of Radhasoami on Guru Movements.* Ph.D. dissertation, University of California at Santa Barbara, 1996.

Drummond, Richard Henry. *A Broader Vision.* Virginia Beach: A.R.E., 1995.

———. *A Life of Jesus the Christ: From Cosmic Origins through the Second Coming.* New York: St. Martin's, 1989.

———. *Unto the Churches: Jesus Christ, Christianity and the Edgar Cayce Readings.* Virginia Beach: A.R.E. Press, 1978.

Ebon, Martin. *Prophecy in Our Time.* New York: New American Library, 1968.

An Edgar Cayce Home Medicine Guide. Virginia Beach: A.R.E., 1982.

Eddy, Sherwood. *You Will Survive After Death.* New York: Rinehart, 1950.

Edwards, Paul. *Reincarnation: A Critical Examination.* Amherst, N. Y.: Prometheus, 1996.

Ericksonian Methods: The Essence of the Story. Jeffrey K. Zeig, ed. New York: Brunner/Mazel, 1994.

Eysenck, Hans. *Astrology: Science or Superstition?* New York: St. Martin's, 1982.

Faivre, Antoine. *Access to Western Esotericism.* Albany: State University of New York Press, 1994.

Festinger, Leon, *et al. When Prophecy Fails.* New York: Harper, 1964.

Fillmore, Charles. *The Twelve Powers of Man.* Unity Village: Unity School of Christianity, n.d.

Fix, William, *et al.* "Keep Digging for Ra Ta." *Venture Inward* 2:5 (September/October 1986), pp. 42–47.

Ford, Arthur. *Nothing So Strange.* New York: Harper & Row, 1958.

Furst, Jeffrey. *Edgar Cayce's Story of Attitudes and Emotions.* New York: Berkley, 1982.

———. *The Return of Frances Willard.* New York: Coward, McCann & Geoghegan, 1971.

Gammon, Margaret. *Astrology and the Edgar Cayce Readings.* Virginia Beach: A.R.E., 1973.

Gardner, Martin. *Fads and Fallacies in the Name of Science.* New York: Dover, 1957.

Godwin, Joscelyn. *Arktos.* Grand Rapids: Phanes, 1993.

Grant, Doris, and Jean Joice. *Food Combining for Health*. Wellingborough: Thorson's, 1984.

The Guideposts Parallel Bible. Carmel, N.Y.: Guideposts, 1981.

Gurdjieff, George I. *Views from the Real World*. New York: Dutton, 1973.

The Handbook for A.R.E. Study Groups. Virginia Beach: A.R.E., 1971.

Heinberg, Richard. "The Lost History of Mankind." *Venture Inward* 12:3 (May/June 1996), p. 48.

Juergensmeyer, Mark. *Radhasoami Reality: The Logic of a Modern Faith*. Princeton: Princeton, 1991.

Jung, Carl. *The Portable Jung*. New York: Penguin, 1971.

Kahn, David E. *My Life with Edgar Cayce*. New York: Doubleday, 1970.

Karp, Reba Ann. *Edgar Cayce Encyclopedia of Healing*. New York: Bantam, 1986.

Kidd, Worth. *Edgar Cayce and Group Dynamics*. Virginia Beach: A.R.E., 1971.

———. *A Way to Fulfillment*. Virginia Beach: A.R.E., 1973.

Krajenke, Robert. *From the Birth of Souls to the Death of Moses*. Virginia Beach: A.R.E., 1989.

Lane, David Christopher. *The Making of a Spiritual Movement: The Untold Story of Paul Twitchell and Eckankar*. 5th ed. Del Mar, California: Del Mar, 1990.

———. *The Radhasoami Tradition: A Critical History of Guru Successorship*. New York: Garland, 1992.

Leary, David M. *Edgar Cayce's Photographic Legacy*. Garden City, N.Y.: Doubleday, 1978.

LeDoux, Joseph. *The Emotional Brain*. New York: Simon & Schuster, 1996.

Lehner, Mark. "Ra Ta: Myth or Reality?" Interview by A. Robert Smith. *Venture Inward* I:4 (March/April 1985), pp. 6–11.

———. "The Search for Ra Ta." Interview by A. Robert Smith. *Venture Inward* I:3 (January/February 1985), pp. 6–11, 47.

McGarey, William A. *The Edgar Cayce Remedies*. New York: Bantam, 1983.

MacNeice, Louis. *Astrology*. Garden City, N.Y.: Doubleday, 1964.

Mack, Burton. *Who Wrote the New Testament?* San Francisco: Harper, 1995.

Mein, Eric A. *Keys to Health: The Promise and Challenge of Holism*. New York: St. Martin's, 1989.

Millard, Joseph. *Edgar Cayce: Mystery Man of Miracles*. New York: Fawcett, 1956.

Miller, Timothy, ed. *America's Alternative Religions.* Albany: State University of New York Press, 1995.

Myss, Caroline. *Anatomy of the Spirit.* New York: Harmony, 1996.

New Bible Commentary: 21st Century Edition. Downers Grove, Ill.: Intervarsity Press, 1994.

Numbers, Ronald. *Prophetess of Health: Ellen G. White and the Origins of Seventh-day Adventist Health Reform.* Knoxville: University of Tennessee Press, 1992.

Pierpaoli, Walter, and William Regelson. *The Melatonin Miracle: Nature's Age-Reversing, Disease-Fighting, Sex-Enhancing Hormone.* New York: Simon & Schuster, 1995.

Podmore, Frank. *From Mesmer to Christian Science.* New York: University Books, 1969.

Prothero, Stephen. *The White Buddhist: The Asian Odyssey of Henry Steel Olcott.* Bloomington: Indiana, 1996.

Purucker, G. de. *Dialogues of G. de Purucker.* Covina: Theosophical University Press, 1948.

————. *Fountain-Source of Occultism.* Pasadena: Theosophical University Press, 1974.

Puryear, Herbert B. *The Edgar Cayce Primer.* New York: Bantam, 1982.

Puryear, Herbert B., and Mark A. Thurston. *Meditation and the Mind of Man.* Virginia Beach: A.R.E., 1975.

Randi, James. *Flim-Flam!: Psychics, ESP, Unicorns and Other Delusions.* Amherst, N.Y.: Prometheus, 1982.

Read, Anne. *Edgar Cayce on Jesus and His Church.* New York: Paperback Library, 1970.

Richards, Douglas. "Did Atlanteans Build the First Pentagon?" *Venture Inward* 2:2 (March/April 1986), pp. 20–24.

Robinson, Lytle. *Edgar Cayce's Story of the Origin and Destiny of Man.* New York: Berkley, 1972.

Rosenfeld, Isadore. *Dr. Rosenfeld's Guide to Alternative Medicine: What Works, What Doesn't—and What's Right for You.* New York: Random House, 1996.

Rowley, Peter. *New Gods in America.* New York: McKay, 1971.

Sakoaian, Frances, and Louis S. Acker. *The Astrologer's Handbook.* New York: Harper & Row, 1974.

Santillana, Giorgio de, and Hertha von Deschend. *Hamlet's Mill.* Boston: Gambit, 1969.

Schoch, Robert M. "The Sphinx: Older by Half?" (interview). *Venture Inward* 8:1 (January/February 1992), pp. 14–17.

A Search for God, Book I. Virginia Beach: A.R.E., 1970.

A Search for God, Book II. Virginia Beach: A.R.E., 1950.

Sechrist, Elsie. *Dreams, Your Magic Mirror.* New York: Cowles, 1968.

Sharma, I. C. *Cayce, Karma, and Reincarnation.* Wheaton: Theosophical Publishing House, 1975.

Singh, Shiv Dayal. *Sar Bachan.* Beas: Radhasoami Satsang, 1974.

Smith, A. Robert. "The Great Pyramid Reveals Her Age." *Venture Inward* 2:3 (May/June 1986), 12–17, 56–57.

———. *Hugh Lynn Cayce: About My Father's Business.* Norfolk/Virginia Beach: Donning, 1988.

———. "Lessons from Heaven's Gate." *Venture Inward* 13:4 (July/August 1997), p. 58.

———. "Schor Claims Discovery of 'Huge Room' Beneath Sphinx." *Venture Inward* 13:5 (September/October 1997), p. 5.

———. "The Sphinx: Older by Half?" (interview with Robert Schoch). *Venture Inward* 8:1 (January/February 1992), pp. 14–17.

Smith, D. Moody. *The Theology of the Gospel of John.* Cambridge: Cambridge University Press, 1995.

Stearn, Jess. *Adventures into the Psychic.* New York: NAL, 1969.

———. *Edgar Cayce—The Sleeping Prophet.* New York: Bantam, 1967.

Steiner, Rudolf. *Life Between Death and Rebirth.* Spring Valley, N.Y.: Anthroposophic Press, 1985.

Sugrue, Thomas. *There is a River.* Virginia Beach: A.R.E., 1973.

Thind, Bhagat Singh. *The House of Happiness.* Salt Lake City: n.p., 1931.

———. *The Radiant Road to Reality: Tested Science of Religion.* New York: n.p., 1939.

———. *Science of Union with God Here and Now: Sat-guru Ka Marag.* Brooklyn: T. Gaus, 1950.

Thurston, Mark, and Christopher Fazel. *The Edgar Cayce Handbook for Creating Your Future.* New York: Ballantine, 1992.

———. *Experiments in a Search for God.* Virginia Beach: A.R.E., 1976.

———. *Visions and Prophecies of a New Age.* Virginia Beach: A.R.E., 1981.

Tillett, Gregory. *The Elder Brother.* London: Routledge & Kegan Paul, 1982.

Todeschi, Kevin. *Edgar Cayce's ESP.* Virginia Beach: A.R.E., 1996.

Versluis, Arthur. *Theosophia: Hidden Dimensions of Christianity.* Hudson, N.Y.: Lindisfarne, 1994.

Wertenbaker, Thomas J. *Norfolk: Historic Southern Port.* Durham, N.C.: Duke, 1962.

Wilber, Ken. *A Brief History of Everything.* Boston: Shambhala, 1996.

Wilson, Colin. *Rudolf Steiner: The Man and His Vision.* Wellingborough: Aquarian Press, 1985.

Wilson, Louis F. *A Universal Pattern of Consciousness.* Hanover, Mass.: Christopher, 1994.

Wuthnow, Robert. *Christianity in the 21st Century.* Oxford: Oxford University Press, 1993.

————, ed. *I Come Away Stronger.* Grand Rapids: Eerdmans, 1994.

123 Questions and Answers from the Edgar Cayce Readings. Virginia Beach: A.R.E., 1974.

Index

Subconscious, 100, 116
Subjective validation, 26
Subjective mind, 117
Submarines, 63
Subtle centers, 125
Sufism, 61
Suggestion, 74
Sugrue, Thomas, 19, 23, 44, 46, 53, 117, 119
Suhrawardi, 61, 125
Summer Rain, Mary, 86
Sunbathing, 22
Superconscious, 99, 100
Surat shabd yoga, 11, 120, 125, 126
Surgery, 14
Survey of eleven doctors, 17
Swedenborg, 28, 105
Switzerland, 89
Syracuse University, 80

Talmud, 75
Telepathy, 21, 133
Temple Beautiful, 65
Temple of Sacrifice, 65
Tertium Organum (Ouspensky), 104, 116, 127
Texas, 6
Theosophers, 37, 43
Theosophical Publishing House, 130
Theosophical Society and movement, 37, 43, 44, 50–52, 109, 110
Theosophists, 23, 47, 50, 54, 55, 77, 106
Theosophy, 1, 2, 6, 11, 30, 31, 33, 37, 43, 44, 47, 50–55, 58, 62, 74, 79, 85, 97, 103, 123, 125
There is a River (Sugrue), 3, 8, 19, 46
Thind, Bhagat Singh, 126–30, 133
Thinking, 108
Third Eye, 121–26
Thomas (apostle), 40
Thurston, Mark, 7, 53, 75, 88, 91–93, 104, 115
Thymus gland, 18, 123, 124
Thyroid gland, 123, 124

Tibet, 6
Tillett, Gregory, 77
Time travel, 61
Time, space and patience, 98
Todeschi, Kevin, 21, 88
Tomatoes, 16
Tomb of Records, 83. *See also* Hall of Records
Tonsillitis, 14
Trance, 105, 132, 133
Transactions of the Blavatsky Lodge, 112
Transiting aspects, 109
Transmutation, 97
Truth and fiction, 11
Twelve Powers of Man (Fillmore), 31
20 Cases Suggestive of Reincarnation (Stevenson), 127
Twitchell, Paul, 127, 133

UFO movement, 32
Unconscious, 105, 106
Unicorns, 61
United Kingdom, 33
United States, 33, 62, 107
Unity School of Christianity, 10, 29–31, 52
Universalism, 39, 48
University of Chicago, 50
University of Pennsylvania, 68
University of Udaipur, 130
Unknown Life of Jesus Christ (Notovitch), 70
Unto the Churches (Drummond), 59
Ur, 38
Uranus, 107, 124

Van Auken, John, 88, 95
Varicose veins, 14
Varieties of Religious Experience (James), 103, 116
Vegetables, 15
Vegetable juices, 14
Vegetarianism, 127